Deep Calls to Deep

The Rev. Peter Savastano, Ph.D. December 3, Covid-19 Turnaround

Deep Calls to Deep

Mysticism, Scripture, and Contemplation

Chad Thralls

ORBIS BOOKS
Maryknoll, New York 10545

The publishing arm of the Maryknoll Fathers and Brothers, Orbis seeks to explore the global dimensions of the Christian faith and mission, to invite dialogue with diverse cultures and religious traditions, and to serve the cause of reconciliation and peace. The books reflect the views of their authors and do not represent the official position of the Maryknoll Society. To learn more about Orbis, visit our website at www.orbisbooks.com.

Library of Congress Cataloging-in-Publication Data

Names: Thralls, Chad, author.

Title: Deep calls to deep : mysticism, scripture, and contemplation / Chad Thralls.

Description: Maryknoll, New York : Orbis Books, 2020. | Includes bibliographical references and index.

Identifiers: LCCN 2020011589 (print) | LCCN 2020011590 (ebook) | ISBN 9781626983984 (trade paperback) | ISBN 9781608338627 (ebook) | ISBN 9781608338627 (ebook)

Subjects: LCSH: Mysticism.

Classification: LCC BV5082.5 .T47 2020 (print) | LCC BV5082.5 (ebook | DDC 248.2/2—dc23

LC record available at https://lccn.loc.gov/2020011589

LC ebook record available at https://lccn.loc.gov/2020011590

Contents

Acknowledgments

Over the years, I have been blessed with many wonderful teachers. The inspiration for this book emerged while I was listening to a homily by Father Michael Holleran. I was fortunate to meet Michael relatively soon after I moved to New York. He had been a Carthusian for twenty-two years before returning to New York to serve as a priest in the archdiocese. Michael is serious about contemplative practice; he leads both a Centering Prayer group at his parish and a Zen meditation group in the city. What is perhaps unique about his ministry is the way he interprets scripture in his preaching. Because his theological formation was in the monastery rather than a seminary) he highlights the mystical elements of the text and those scriptural themes that fundamentally connect us to God. In part, this book is an attempt to explain how we can approach scripture as Michael does so that we can experience this connection ourselves. It is also an expression of gratitude for bringing an emphasis on the mystical element of Christianity into ordinary parish life.

Introduction

What is the point of religion? What motivates our religious practices and church activities? This book argues that being religious is not simply a matter of believing in something in order to score points with the Rule Keeper to gain entry to the afterlife. Nor is the primary purpose of religious communities to raise money, maintain a building, create community, care for people, or even engage in mission. Rather, the point of being religious and belonging to a religious community is to cultivate awareness of the presence of God and to be transformed by that encounter. Any "religious" action should be a response to such a growth in awareness.

This perspective is echoed by Evelyn Underhill (1875–1941) in a letter she wrote to Archbishop Lang of Canterbury, a copy of which was found among her papers after she died. In this letter she presented to the bishops of the Anglican Communion for the upcoming Lambeth Conference of 1930 what she thought should be the first duty of the priest. Speaking of the church, she wrote:

Her deepest need is a renewal, first in the clergy and through them in the laity, of the great Christian tradition of the inner life. The Church wants not more consecrated philanthropists, but a disciplined priesthood of theocentric souls who shall be tools and channels of the Spirit of God: and this she cannot have until Communion with God is recognized as the first duty of the priest.

She continues:

God is the interesting thing about religion, and people are hungry for God. But only a priest whose life is soaked in prayer, sacrifice, and love can, by his own spirit of adoring worship, help us to apprehend Him. . . . However difficult and apparently unrewarding, care for the interior spirit is the first duty of every priest. Divine renewal can only come through those whose roots are in the world of prayer.[1]

By arguing for the importance of the inner life, I am not promoting a quaint medieval curiosity, an antiquated relic better left in historical texts on dusty library shelves. On the contrary, the inner life, as Underhill advocates, is an integral part of the religious enterprise. Early twentieth-century British scholar Friedrich von Hügel specifically

---

[1] Evelyn Underhill, "A Letter from Evelyn Underhill to Archbishop Lang of Canterbury," http://www.anglicanlibrary.org/underhill/UnderhillLettertoArchbishopLangofCanterbury.pdf.

addresses this point. For von Hügel, there are three elements always present in any religious tradition. The first is the institutional element. This includes the physical buildings, priests and ministers, hierarchy of leadership, creeds, traditions, and rules that communities of faith have followed throughout their history. The second is the intellectual element. Theology fundamentally is "faith seeking understanding." The intellectual element of a religion attempts to make sense of inherited scriptures and doctrines in dialogue with the contemporary world. This work is done in universities, seminaries, and church fellowship halls. The third element is the experiential or mystical. Von Hügel writes, "Here religion is rather felt than seen or reasoned about, is loved and lived rather than analyzed, is action and power, rather than external fact or intellectual verification."[2] For von Hügel, all three elements are essential in any healthy religious tradition. When any of the three is missing, an imbalance occurs that impoverishes the whole.[3] This means that the mystical is not a fringe element of religion. Contrary to those who emphasize one element of religious life at the expense of the other two, the mystical is an essential element of religion, and the tradition misses a dynamic source of life and vitality when it is omitted.

---

[2] Friedrich von Hügel, *The Mystical Element of Religion: As Studied in Saint Catherine of Genoa and Her Friends* (New York: Crossroad, 1999), 53.

[3] Dennis Tamburello, *Ordinary Mysticism* (Mahwah, NJ: Paulist Press, 1996), 21.

Today, many are moving away from institutional religion. The "nones"—those unaffiliated with traditional religious communities—are on the rise.[4] This is due, in part, to religion being distracted from its main purpose—connecting with the Divine. When religion is used to divide people or is reduced to a political platform, many conclude that its primary purpose has been abandoned. German theologian Karl Rahner (1904–84), writes: "The devout Christian of the future will either be a 'mystic,' one who has 'experienced' something, or he will cease to be anything at all."[5] This suggests that we must either stop using religion as a vehicle for things for which it was not intended or risk losing it entirely. Fundamentally, Rahner's claim indicates that we should not neglect the mystical because it is an essential element of religion.

Interest in mysticism has risen dramatically over the past fifty years. Most treatments of the mystical element of Christianity address this phenomenon through historical figures and their writings. The text most Christians understand their faith through, however, is the Bible. Therefore, our main objective is to explain the central themes of Christian mysticism through this primary mystical text. This approach is fitting because the original understanding of the term *mystical* referred to the search for hidden

---

[4] See Elizabeth Drescher, *Choosing Our Religion: The Spiritual Lives of America's Nones* (New York: Oxford University Press, 2016).

[5] Karl Rahner, "Christian Living Formerly and Today," in *Theological Investigations* VII, trans. David Bourke (Herder and Herder, 1971), 15

meaning in scripture. It described the insights uncovered by those who discovered God's word for them personally. Our goal is to show how a mystical approach to Christian faith through an exploration of biblical passages, the teachings of a variety of mystics, and practices such as contemplation cultivates intimacy with God, which, in turn, can help readers experience mystical consciousness for themselves.

Note, however, that this is not a book of biblical scholarship; neither will it attempt to address the whole of scripture. We will focus on specific biblical texts that evocatively convey aspects of the phenomenon of mysticism. Furthermore, we will incorporate the insights of scholars and practitioners to understand better the mystical element of Christianity and how it is practiced. Finally, we will explore how mystics read the Bible, their understanding of God and what it means to be human, their descriptions of religious experience, and how they relate to their fellow human beings and the natural world. In the process we will glimpse how to reapproach the Bible after years of reading it through an overly historical lens and discover in the mystics a profound resource for contemporary Christians as they live out their faith today. As we proceed, the case will be made that Christianity is fundamentally a mystical tradition that is most fruitfully approached from this perspective.

1

What Is Mysticism?

The mystical element in Christianity is partly an antidote to the publicly divisive and political representation of the tradition today. However, before we explore this approach, we need to address our current cultural moment. Institutional religion is in decline, while the number of "nones"—those who do not identify with a religious tradition—is increasing. At the same time, contemplative practices such as mindfulness and yoga are becoming more popular. Mindfulness, the practice of intentionally paying attention to the present moment without judgment, draws significant corporate and therapeutic interest. There are numerous psychological studies that demonstrate the effectiveness of mindfulness in treating mental-health problems. For example, Traci Pedersen notes that short-term group mindfulness-based therapy was just as effective, and less expensive, as more traditional talk therapy and medication in treating patients with anxiety, depression, and adjustment disorders.[1]

While popular interest in mindfulness will probably wane with the advent of the next healthy lifestyle trend, the benefits it provides are significant and quantifiable. Studies have demonstrated a variety of positive outcomes, such as helping to understand mental and physical pain, sharpening attention, lowering stress, and reducing brain chatter.[2]

So, why even consider Christian mysticism when many today find mindfulness so beneficial? First, without diminishing the benefits of mindfulness and its usefulness in refocusing after getting lost in one's thoughts, especially negative ones, it should be noted that pioneering figures like Jon Kabat-Zinn pulled mindfulness out of the Buddhist tradition, which provides a wider understanding of how to live a meaningful life than the secular practice of mindfulness. Certainly, mindfulness can help lower stress level and discourage one from ruminating on negative thoughts, but it cannot provide an overall shape or direction to one's life. Like Buddhism, the Christian mystical tradition has much to offer in terms of structuring a life filled with meaning and purpose beyond decreased brain chatter and increased powers of attention, though these

---

[1] Traci Pedersen, "Mindfulness Group Therapy Can Be as Good as Individual CBT for Many Psychiatric Symptoms," *Psych Central* (April 17, 2017; updated August 8, 2018).

[2] "Getting Started with Mindfulness," http://www.mindful.org.

physical manifestations may be side effects of a sustained practice of contemplative prayer.

Second, instead of utilizing mindfulness to understand the causes of our mental suffering and the suffering caused by the institutions in which we participate, it is often used simply as a technique to calm the self and become more productive at work. Consequently, it can easily become a tool to promote individualistic consumerism.[3] When packaged this way, mindfulness reinforces the neoliberal status quo when it could be a means of transforming it.

Just as mindfulness and yoga demonstrate the popular appeal of contemplative practice, Christian mysticism too offers inner peace to those who are stressed or anxious. As Jesus says, "Come to me, all you that are weary and are carrying heavy burdens, and I will give you rest. Take my yoke upon you, and learn from me; for I am gentle and humble in heart, and you will find rest for your souls. For my yoke is easy, and my burden is light" (Mt 11:28–30).

Introductions to the topic of Christian mysticism usually emphasize the ideas of the official canon of classic mystical writers. The great mystics certainly can help us understand different themes in the tradition, but this book uses as its primary source the mystical text that Christians already read, the Bible. As we proceed, we explore essential

---

[3] Mark McIntosh, *Mystical Theology: The Integrity of Spirituality and Theology* (Malden, MA: Blackwell, 1998), 10, 69; see also Ronald Purser, *McMindfulness: How Mindfulness Became the New Capitalist Spirituality* (London: Repeater Books, 2019).

themes such as how mystics read the Bible, how they understand who God is and how we are related to God, how
to practice contemplative prayer, how mystics respond to
encountering God, and how they relate to God through
the natural world.

The first two chapters provide a foundation for our
journey. In this chapter we explore some classic and contemporary definitions of mysticism and make the case for
why Christian mysticism is so relevant today. The goal
of this project is to demystify mysticism and make this
element of Christianity accessible to a wider audience
so that people can benefit from the wisdom it offers for
understanding and practicing their faith.

DEFINITIONS

The term *mysticism* popularly denotes something mysterious, paranormal, or just plain weird. In the study of
religion it has a more specific meaning. To understand the
term better, let's consider four points from recent scholarship. The contemporary scholar who has brought the
most clarity to the study of Christian mysticism is Bernard
McGinn. He defines a mystic as one who is "committed
to the search for a deeper contact with God."[4] Striking
a similar note, Mark McIntosh defines spirituality "as

---

[4] Bernard McGinn, "What Is a Mystic?" interview (May 21, 2013),
https://www.youtube.com/watch?v=g7uHZUJ3_VI.

the new and transformative pattern of life and thought engendered in people by their encounter with God."[5] William Harmless also emphasizes that mysticism is the experiential aspect of religion. He defines it as "a domain of religion that deals with the search for and the attainment of a profound experiential knowledge of God or of ultimate reality."[6] Simply put, though McGinn prefers the less philosophically problematic term *consciousness* to *experience,* our first point is that *mysticism concerns the cultivation of a deep and transformative awareness of the presence of God.*[7]

A second point, as Harmless suggests, is that *mystical experience imparts knowledge to the mystic.* To describe such knowledge of God, he shares the definition proposed by Jean Gerson (1363–1429): "Mystical theology is an experiential knowledge of God that comes through the embrace of unitive love."[8] Knowledge of God is obviously different from scientific knowledge. Harmless compares it to the knowledge spouses have of each other.

---

[5] McIntosh, *Mystical Theology*, 9. Mysticism is a specialization within the discipline of spirituality, which studies lived religious experience more broadly.

[6] William Harmless, *Mystics* (New York: Oxford University Press, 2008), 263.

[7] Bernard McGinn, "Introduction," in *The Essential Writings of Christian Mysticism* (New York: Modern Library, 2006), xv–xvi. For a detailed treatment of this point, see Bernard McGinn, "Mystical Consciousness: A Modest Proposal," *Spiritus* 8, no. 1 (2008): 44–63.

[8] In Harmless, *Mystics*, 5.

[Married people] have not read books about one another. They have not studied each other academically. They know one another through the union of their lives, an intimacy that touches heart and mind and body. There is certainly a cognitive element in their knowledge of each other, but it is not what we would call intellectual knowledge. It is certainly not theoretical.[9]

The mystical element reminds our scientific age that there are different types of knowing. Knowledge of God is a love-knowledge that is illustrated beautifully in Blaise Pascal's aphorism: "The heart has its reasons of which reason knows nothing."[10]

Bernard McGinn highlights a third point in his formal academic definition of mysticism. He writes:

The mystical element in Christianity is that part of its beliefs and practices that concerns the preparation for, the consciousness of, and the reaction to what can be described as the immediate or direct presence of God.[11]

In this definition McGinn insists that mysticism, properly conceived, includes more than just powerful experiences.

---

[9] Harmless, *Mystics*, 6.

[10] Blaise Pascal, *Pensees*, trans. A. J. Krailsheimer (New York: Penguin Classics, 1995), 127, no. 423.

[11] McGinn, *Essential Writings*, xiv.

Mysticism is more than just a new feeling; it is *a process, journey, or way of life.* All the mystic's discipline and training in preparation to receive such an experience, as well as the transformed life that is a fruit of the encounter, are properly understood as mystical. When we talk about mysticism, we are not simply interested in experiences, no matter how profound. Mysticism is not about temporary states, but the entire itinerary the mystic follows in his or her journey to God.

Our fourth point is that mysticism is not only for a select few religious elite. Until 1200 CE, Christian mysticism was primarily a monastic phenomenon. A significant benefit of the twentieth-century revival of interest in mysticism is that its teaching and practice have moved beyond the walls of monasteries and become accessible to many more people. There is now a much greater availability of mystical texts in translation than ever before. While these texts can greatly improve one's understanding of mysticism, one's own experience can seem paltry in comparison. McGinn addresses this concern with the example of basketball. He notes that despite the fact that greats such as Michael Jordan and LeBron James play at an extraordinarily high level, many others enjoy playing the game as well and look up to these legends as examples to emulate.[12] He then explains that, like basketball, the mystical element of religion is for everyone:

---

[12] McGinn, "What Is a Mystic?"

I think the best way to look at mysticism is to speak of it as the search for a deeper awareness and consciousness of God's presence in your life. And that's the original meaning of the word "mystic," which means "hidden." God is hidden in everything—hidden in us, hidden in the world. And the mystic is the person who is seeking to find God, the God who is often hidden, in a deeper and a more transformative way. So in that sense mysticism is really an integral part of religion. It's not some kind of very *special* thing for a *few* people. I think every baptized Christian is called to find God as deeply as they can in their own lives, and that's what I think mysticism is.[13]

For McGinn, though we will never exhibit the greatness of a LeBron James, all of us can become mystics if we prepare ourselves by putting in the practice.

THE RELEVANCE OF MYSTICISM

As noted earlier, with regard to the state of contemporary religious life, three narratives stand out: First, institutional religion is in decline and the "nones" are on the increase. In her study of this group Elizabeth Drescher found that nones, despite their lack of affiliation, engage in a variety

---

[13] Bernard McGinn, "What Is Mysticism?" interview (May 21, 2013), https://www.youtube.com/watch?v=3bwLUiZj1Tk.

of spiritual practices.[14] Second, those who remain affiliated with religious communities are divided between those who want clear definitions of morality and unambiguous standards of community participation, and those who seek to include groups that have historically been marginalized. Third, contemplative practices such as mindfulness and yoga are becoming more popular.

On a personal level, everyday life is fast paced, demanding, and stressful; thoughts and questions continually bombard the psyche. How am I going to get all of this work done? Am I doing enough to advance my career? Am I spending enough time with my family? Do I spend my money wisely? Was I there for my friends when they needed me? Beyond these questions, barely conscious psychological needs for things like order, security, control, and perfection also create anxiety.

Christian mysticism is relevant for such a cultural moment and for several reasons. First, as the popularity of contemplative practices such as mindfulness and yoga attest, even though institutional religion is out of fashion, the desire to be centered is not. Second, the mystical element specifically addresses the anxiety that attracts people to yoga, and religious communities are the logical places to find training in these disciplines. Despite this, I've rarely heard sermons on mysticism or how to cultivate

---

[14] Elizabeth Drescher, *Choosing Our Religion: The Spiritual Lives of America's Nones* (New York: Oxford University Press, 2016).

an awareness of God's presence. Even though there have
been Christian mystics since the second century, their
approach to faith, including the way they read and interpret scripture, is not well known. Third, many are tired of
religion spending its energy identifying who is numbered
among the sheep and the goats rather than calling people
to what is deepest in life. Instead of dividing humanity into
the children of light and children of darkness, mysticism
eschews dualities. It invites us to see the connections between human beings and God, the connections among our
fellow human beings, and the interdependence between
human beings and the natural world. Finally, mysticism
produces tangible effects that religious *beliefs* cannot. We
live in a scientific age. Our contemporaries are skeptical
of all claims that cannot be supported by evidence. When
applied, mysticism provides a path that can cultivate interior stillness for oneself.

I hope that the mystical element in Christianity has
intrigued you enough to want to learn more. Let us now
consider how mystics read and interpret scripture.

2

The Spiritual Interpretation of Scripture

Reading scripture is a fundamental practice for any Christian seeking to grow in faith. Understanding scripture, however, is not simple and straightforward; there are multiple lenses through which one can interact with the text. This chapter explores how mystics read the Bible. But we must first acknowledge that the way we read texts today differs from the way the great mystics of the past did so. One significant difference is that most of the reading people do today is not on a printed page but online. Nicholas Carr explores this phenomenon, examining his reading habits and how they have changed since the arrival of the internet.[1] Previously, he had been able to sit down with a challenging book and read it without much distraction. Now, he loses focus after a few pages. He argues that the way we use the internet—the skimming we

---

[1] Nicholas Carr, "Is Google Making Us Stupid?: What the Internet Is Doing to Our Brains," *Atlantic* (July/August 2008).

do online—has changed our ability to pay attention. Carr is not against technology; his point is that, although the internet is a great way to obtain information, the way we often use it decreases our ability to concentrate and focus on the text we are reading.

Another contrast between how we read texts now and how a mystic reads the scriptures is that the latter reads as a lover might read. Today, we read mostly to gain information. We do so rapidly, and when we have finished an article, we quickly move on to the next one. Paul Griffiths notes that we read different types of texts in varying ways. For example, we read the newspaper very differently from the way we read a letter from someone we love. To describe the difference, Griffiths distinguishes between consumerist reading and religious reading.[2] After we have read a newspaper or magazine, for example, we throw it away. We don't save or reread old newspapers. At most, we might bookmark an article in our web browser. Consumerist reading, therefore, is disposable. Religious reading, on the other hand, is akin to reading a love letter. Those precious few times we receive such a letter, we savor the words. We read them slowly. And when we reach the end, we immediately go back to the beginning and start reading again. Religious reading, therefore, entails a different relationship to what is being read. To read something religiously is to

---

[2] Paul Griffiths, *Religious Reading: The Place of Reading in the Practice of Religion* (New York: Oxford University Press, 1999), 41–42.

expect a text that is a "vastly rich resource, one that yields meaning, suggestions (or imperatives) for action, matter for aesthetic wonder, and much else. It is a treasure house, an ocean, a mine: the deeper religious readers dig . . . the greater will be their reward."[3] To read religiously is to read not for information but for transformation. Religious readers approach the text with reverence.[4] For them, there is no final act of reading. The text has something new to offer each time they return to it.[5]

ORIGEN OF ALEXANDRIA

The Christian mystic whose method of reading scripture has been the most influential is Origen of Alexandria (184–253 CE). In Book IV of *On First Principles* he explains his basic approach to reading the Bible. For Origen, all scripture is divinely inspired. No matter the genre of literature (whether commandment, genealogy, or historical narrative), all scripture communicates Christ to the believer.[6] Origen writes, "We cannot say of the Holy Spirit's writings that there is anything useless or unnecessary in them, however much they appear useless to some.

---

[3] Griffiths, *Religious Reading*, 41.

[4] Griffiths, *Religious Reading,* 42.

[5] Griffiths, *Religious Reading*, 41.

[6] Rowan Greer, trans., *Origen: An Exhortation to Martyrdom, Prayer, and Selected Works* (New York: Paulist Press, 1979), 177.

What we ought rather to do is turn the eyes of our mind toward him who ordered this to be written and to ask of him their meaning."[7] In some passages the meaning of the words is clear. Origen refers to this as the ordinary or narrative meaning of the passage.[8] The meaning of other passages, however, is more obscure. Anyone who has spent much time reading the Bible knows there are many passages that do not seem to have a spiritual purpose, nor make literal sense.[9] About such passages, Origen claims:

> Divine wisdom has arranged for there to be certain stumbling blocks or interruptions of the narrative meaning, by inserting in its midst certain impossibilities and contradictions, so that the very interruption of the narrative might oppose the reader, as it were, with certain obstacles thrown in the way. By then wisdom denies a way and an access to the common understanding; and when we are shut out and hurled back, it calls us back to the beginning of another way, so that by gaining a higher and loftier road through entering a narrow footpath it may open for us the immense breadth of divine knowledge.[10]

---

[7] Quoted in Louis Dupre and James Wiseman, eds., "Origen (c.185–c.253)," in *Light from Light: An Anthology of Christian Mysticism*, 2nd ed. (New York: Paulist Press, 2001), 29.

[8] Greer, *Origen*, 182, 184.

[9] Greer, *Origen*, 188.

[10] Greer, *Origen*, 187–88.

According to Origen, the Holy Spirit incorporated these difficult passages into scripture to force readers to look for another way to understand God's message.

Origen sought to read the scriptures more deeply because, he believed, there is an inexhaustible depth to them. For him, no one can ever understand them fully.[11] To illustrate the depth of meaning present in the biblical text, he quotes scripture itself: "The kingdom of heaven is like treasure hidden in a field, which someone found and hid; then in his joy he goes and sells all that he has and buys that field" (Mt 13:44).[12] To explain how these hidden treasures relate to the narrative of the text, Origen borrows a distinction found in 2 Corinthians 3:6, where the apostle Paul contrasts the letter and the spirit of the law. Origen takes this distinction and applies it to the text itself; for him, the letter of the text is its literal meaning. The literal sense of scripture is the meaning intended by the original author.[13] The spirit of the text, in contrast, is the hidden or spiritual meaning of the passage. This level of meaning is not unintentional, not an afterthought. It was deliberately included in the text by the Holy Spirit. For Origen, the aim of the Holy Spirit "is to envelop and hide secret mysteries in ordinary words under the pretext

---

[11] Greer, *Origen*, 202–3.

[12] Greer, *Origen*, 198–99.

[13] Raymund Studzinski, *Reading to Live: The Evolving Practice of* Lectio Divina, Cistercian Publications (Collegeville, MN: Liturgical Press, 2009), 31, 55.

of a narrative of some kind and of an account of visible things."[14] Note, however, that the secrets hidden in the text are not gnostic or esoteric truths reserved for an elite few. Rather, the Holy Spirit hides spiritual meaning under the letter of the text so the diligent reader seeking God's word through the text can find it.

This means that mystics aren't simply interested in what a particular text means in its original context, as important as this is. Such readers approach the text seeking to know what this text has to say to them. Whatever the text is saying literally, mystics ask themselves: Is there a road here that I need to travel? Is there a river I need to cross? Are there aspects of the self or ego that I need to stop clinging to? Or patterns of thoughts I need to watch carefully? For the mystic, *we* are the field in which the treasure has been hidden. We must turn within, like the merchant in search of fine pearls, in order to find it (cf. Mt 13:45–46). Therefore, the mystic's fundamental principle of spiritual interpretation is: "Whatever is happening in this passage has to do with me. How can I realize what is being said in the text within myself?" One of the most influential verses in the contemplative tradition can be found in Galatians: "It is no longer I who live, but it is Christ who lives in me" (2:20). Illustrating this mystical principle of interpretation, Father Michael Holleran often says to those who hear him preach: "You are the temple. You are the New

---

[14] Greer, *Origen*, 187.

Jerusalem. You are the Christ."[15] Holleran doesn't mean that we are literally a building or a city. He is interpreting the text mystically and encouraging his congregation to experience the reality the verse in Galatians points to for themselves.

TWO CONTEMPORARY CHALLENGES

For contemporary readers Origen's distinction between letter and spirit presents two challenges to reading like a mystic. The first challenge is fundamentalism. The fundamentalist insists that the only possible interpretation of the biblical text is the literal one. Consequently, because the only meaning the text can have is the face value, common-sense meaning of the words, there are severe limitations on what can be gleaned from the text. Such an approach is *not* one to which early Christians subscribed. For example, in a discussion of how scripture should be interpreted, Origen lists examples of verses in the first four chapters of Genesis that should not be taken literally:

> To what person of intelligence, I say, will the account seem logically consistent that says there was a "first day" and a "second" and "third," in which also "evening" and "morning" are named, without a sun, without a moon, and without stars. . . . But there is

---

[15] For an extensive collection of Holleran's homilies, see https://www.youtube.com/user/FrCarthusian.

> no need for us to enlarge the discussion too much
> beyond what we have in hand, since it is quite easy
> for everyone who wishes to collect from the holy
> Scriptures things that are written as though they
> were really done, but cannot be believed to have
> happened appropriately and reasonably according to
> the narrative meaning.[16]

Unlike the fundamentalist, however, the mystic understands that there are multiple layers of meaning to a text.
Origen maintains that logically problematic texts like the
creation narratives are included in the text not to be interpreted literally but rather to guide the reader toward a
spiritual interpretation of the passage. Interpreting the text
spiritually requires openness to what the text can reveal,
but promises rich rewards to the reader who seeks God's
message through it.

A second contemporary challenge presented by
Origen's distinction occurs when the historical-critical
method of interpretation eclipses other ways of reading
the text. Since the Enlightenment and the rise of critical
scholarship in the humanities, scholars have asked questions about the date, authorship, audience, and purpose of
the various writings within sacred scripture. In doing so
they have increased our understanding of the Bible signifi-
cantly. For example, based on this valuable scholarship, it
is not sufficient simply to read the text at face value. One

---

16 Greer, *Origen*, 189.

must *interpret* the text and, in coming to understand the text's meaning, one must consider its historical context.

Based on the work of Paul Ricoeur, Sandra Schneiders identifies three aspects of the process of interpretation: wrestling with the world *behind* the text (history); the world *of* the text (language); and the world *before* the text (the appropriation by the reader).[17] Each of these aspects is necessary for a full engagement with scripture. Reading the Bible with *only* a historical or linguistic lens inhibits the process of interpretation because it limits the ability of the text to speak to the personal life of the reader.

THE SPIRITUAL RICHNESS OF SCRIPTURE

Origen sought to encounter Christ throughout the entire Bible, even in texts that don't at first seem fruitful for devotional reading. To unlock the spiritual richness of scripture, one needs to move beyond the literal meaning in search of the spirit of the text. In other words, in one's search for buried treasure in scripture, one might interpret biblical stories as allegories, as Paul does in the allegory of Hagar and Sarah in Galatians 4.[18] Beneath their literal meaning, Origen is interested in what the particular details of biblical stories might represent and have to say to the reader in the moment of reading.

---

[17] Sandra M. Schneiders, *The Revelatory Text: Interpreting the New Testament as Sacred Scripture*, 2nd ed. (Collegeville, MN: Michael Glazer, 1999).

[18] Greer, *Origen*, 185.

The Song of Songs in the Hebrew scriptures illustrates how mystics have approached the biblical text. Interestingly, the word *God* does not appear in the book. Its eight chapters are a racy love poem between a bride and bridegroom (for example, see Song 7). Early Christian authors interpreted the bridegroom as God and the bride as the church. Origen was the first exegete who read the text as a love poem between Christ and the individual soul.[19]

Many Christian mystics have written commentaries on the Song of Songs. For example, Bernard of Clairvaux (1090–1153) began writing a series of sermons on the book in 1135 and continued intermittently until his death.[20] He wrote eighty-six in all. Like Origen before him, Bernard read the book as an allegory depicting the passionate love between God and the soul. One of the images in the text that captivated him was the kiss. For example, the bride declares, "Let him kiss me with the kisses of his mouth" (Song 1:2). For Bernard, the bride is the soul that thirsts for God.[21] The kiss of the Bridegroom is a taste of the experience of God's love. It is a momentary union of God with the human person.[22] It is the sweetness

---

[19] Origen, "Commentary on the Song of Songs," in *The Essential Writings of Christian Mysticism*, ed. Bernard McGinn (New York: Modern Library, 2006), 6.

[20] Gillian Evans, *Bernard of Clairvaux: Selected Works* (Mahwah, NJ: Paulist Press, 1987), 209.

[21] Evans, *Bernard of Clairvaux*, 231.

[22] Evans, *Bernard of Clairvaux*, 217.

of the Holy Spirit.[23] Once the bride tastes it, her desire is kindled; there is no end to it. She seeks to satisfy it again and again.[24]

In Sermons 3 and 4, Bernard interprets the kiss as a series of stages on the spiritual journey. At the beginning of the journey the soul is "burdened with sins."[25] Because of its sinfulness, at the first stage the soul "may not rashly lift his face to the face of the most serene Bridegroom, but he can throw himself timidly at the feet of the most severe Lord."[26] Through repentance, the soul prostrates itself and humbly kisses the feet of the Bridegroom. The second stage is an intermediate one. Pleased by the soul's repentance, the Bridegroom extends a hand and lifts it up. In gratitude, the soul responds to this grace by kissing the hand of the Bridegroom. In this stage God provides grace and assistance to the soul, which empowers it to grow in holiness and progress on the journey. In the third stage, the soul receives the long-desired kiss of the Beloved on the mouth. With this kiss, "the presence of him who forgives, the benefactor, is experienced as strongly as it can be in a fragile body."[27] Bernard says this experience is rare, "given only to the perfect," but it is one in which "we are made one with him in spirit through his kindness."[28]

---

[23] Evans, *Bernard of Clairvaux*, 221.

[24] Evans, *Bernard of Clairvaux*, 221, 274.

[25] Evans, *Bernard of Clairvaux*, 221.

[26] Evans, *Bernard of Clairvaux*, 221.

[27] Evans, *Bernard of Clairvaux*, 225.

[28] Evans, *Bernard of Clairvaux*, 224, 223.

READING LIKE A MYSTIC

Writers such as Origen affirm that God may be encountered through reading the Bible. The monastic practice of reading scripture is called *lectio divina* (sacred reading). Over the centuries spiritual writers have conceptualized this method in various ways; perhaps the most famous description is found in *The Ladder of Monks* by Guigo II (d. 1188). This treatise breaks *lectio divina* into a series of four steps that proceed from *reading*, to *meditation* (in this context using reason to reflect on the meaning of the passage), to petitionary *prayer*, and finally to the gift of *contemplation*. In summary, he states, "Reading, as it were, puts food whole into the mouth, meditation chews it and breaks it up, prayer extracts its flavor, contemplation is the sweetness itself which gladdens and refreshes. Reading works on the outside, meditation on the pith; prayer asks for what we long for, contemplation gives us delight in the sweetness which we have found."[29]

When we read something to gain information, speed is advantageous. When we read for transformation, it is important to take our time. Ewert Cousins (1927–2009) states that in monastic reading the monks' goal "was not to finish a passage, but to enter prayerfully into its depths by dwelling on a sentence, a phrase, or even a word—mulling

---

[29] Guigo II, *The Ladder of Monks and Twelve Meditations*, trans. Edmund Colledge and James Walsh (Kalamazoo, MI: Cistercian Publications, 1981), 69.

it over, ruminating on it, allowing it to sink into their being and resonate on many levels of meaning."[30] Similarly, Dietrich Bonhoeffer (1906–45) states:

> Whereas in our devotions together we read long consecutive passages, in our personal meditation we confine ourselves to a brief selected text, which possibly may not be changed for a whole week. If in our reading of the Scriptures together we are led into the whole length and breadth of the Bible, here we go into the unfathomable depths of a particular sentence and word. . . . In our meditation we ponder the chosen text on the strength of the promise that it has something utterly personal to say to us for this day and for our Christian life, that it is not only God's Word for the Church, but also God's Word for us individually. We expose ourselves to the specific word until it addresses us personally. . . . It is not necessary that we should get through the entire passage in one meditation. Often we shall have to stop with one sentence or even one word, because we have been gripped and arrested and cannot evade it any longer.[31]

---

[30] Ewert Cousins, "The Fourfold Sense of Scripture in Christian Mysticism," in *Mysticism and Sacred Scripture*, ed. Steven Katz (New York: Oxford University Press, 2000), 124.

[31] Dietrich Bonhoeffer, *Life Together* (New York: Harper and Row, 1954), 81–83.

Consequently, to read like a mystic means to choose a short passage of scripture; to read it slowly, expecting God to speak through it; and to know that one can return to it again and again without ever exhausting the spiritual meaning available within it.

The importance of reading slowly returns us to the theme with which we started. We began by describing two differences between the way we read texts today and the way mystics read the scriptures. Environmental scientist David Orr makes a distinction between "fast knowledge" and "slow knowledge" that illustrates the importance of taking our time. For him, fast knowledge rests on the fundamental assumptions that drive contemporary technology and commerce, such as new knowledge is better than old knowledge; we always need to be acquiring more new knowledge; knowledge that is valuable is knowledge that is useful; and we are capable of retrieving the right bit of knowledge at the right time to solve problems.[32] A contemporary buzzword associated with this mentality is *disruption*. For Orr, the problem with the acquisition and application of new knowledge is that many of the intractable problems that currently plague society—such as the development and use of fossil fuels, nuclear weapons, high-input agriculture, and the demands of short-term economic growth—have been caused by "knowledge acquired and applied before we had time to think it through

---

[32] David Orr, "Slow Knowledge," in *Hope Is an Imperative: The Essential David Orr* (Washington, DC: Island Press, 2010), 14.

clearly."[33] Slow knowledge, in contrast, is more patient. It recognizes that humans assimilate new knowledge slowly and that it takes time to consider the implications of what has been discovered. Orr does not oppose the discovery of new knowledge. There are undeniable benefits of technological innovation in many areas of life, but he claims that knowledge is different from wisdom. Regarding our present discussion, spiritual wisdom is not a product of how much of the Bible we have read or studied, or sermon ideas we have gleaned from our reading, but rather whether we have slowed down and taken the time to listen to the word of God that lies hidden beneath the text.

---

[33] Orr, "Slow Knowledge," 15.

3

Mystical Discourse

IMAGES OF GOD

Fundamentally, God is mystery. As Saint Paul states, "How unsearchable are his judgments and how inscrutable his ways!" (Rom 11:33). It is not possible for human beings to understand the essence of God. Nevertheless, people throughout history have experienced this elusive depth of existence, and, not content to remain ignorant of this mysterious "Other," humanity has assigned various qualities to God to bring this unknown reality into relationship. Christians receive knowledge about the character of God through images and symbols found in scripture, liturgy, and tradition. These images and symbols help us understand an aspect of the character of God. For example, the masculine images used in the liturgy, such as in the Our Father and the trinitarian language of the Nicene Creed, help Christians understand who God is and how to relate to God.

Sandra Schneiders claims that one of the main tools scripture employs is metaphor. For Schneiders, "a genuine metaphor is characterized by linguistic tension between a literally absurd statement and that to which it points. The literal absurdity of the statement forces the mind to seek for meaning at a deeper level."[1] For example, Schneiders notes that there is linguistic tension in the biblical depiction of God as father:

It is literally absurd to say that God is our father. A father is a male human being who has engendered a child by sexual intercourse with a human female. Obviously, nothing in this literal definition can be applied to God who is not a human being, does not have male sexual organs, does not have intercourse with human females, and does not have children by physical generation. Since the statement "God is our father" is obviously intended to carry meaning, the mind must seek meaning at another level. The reason we use a metaphor is that we have no other way to speak concretely of God. The reason we use this particular metaphor is that the human experience of fatherhood (and of certain other realities) has something in common with our God-experience and we realize that by using the metaphor we can tease the mind into creative reflection on the mysterious God.[2]

---

[1] Sandra Schneiders, *Women and the Word: The Gender of God in the New Testament and the Spirituality of Women* (Mahwah, NJ: Paulist Press, 1986), 25.

[2] Schneiders, *Women and the Word*, 25–26.

In addition to the metaphor of father, scripture uses many other metaphors to describe the character of God, including ones from nature, such as sun, light, fire, rock, and fountain of living water. Others use human roles to tell us something about God, such as "potter, builder, shepherd, hero, warrior, physician, midwife, homemaker, judge, and king."[3] While they are outnumbered by male metaphors or roles occupied mostly by men in the cultures that produced the texts of scripture, Schneiders emphasizes that feminine images of God are also present. These latter are often maternal images that depict God as giving birth or caring for and nurturing children.[4] An example is found in the Book of Isaiah:

> Can a woman forget her nursing child,
>   or show no compassion for the child
>   of her womb?
> Even these may forget,
>   yet I will not forget you. (Isa 49:15)

As we noted in the previous chapter, Christian mystics, like Bernard of Clairvaux, have used the imagery of bride and bridegroom from the Song of Songs to describe the relationship between God and the soul. Bridal (or erotic) mysticism was a movement in thirteenth-century Europe that built on this imagery. One of the most interesting

---

[3] Schneiders, *Women and the Word*, 26.

[4] Feminine images are found in, for example, Deuteronomy 32:18, Isaiah 66:13, and Psalm 131:2.

writers in the movement was the thirteenth-century mystic Mechthild of Magdeburg. Her writing is filled with metaphors. She wedded images from the court life of the medieval German nobility to those of the Song of Songs to describe the relationship between God and the soul. For Mechthild, God is the Lord of the heavenly court. Angels are the dukes and servants of the court. The soul is the bride exiled here on earth due to the fall of humankind. Because the Lord desires his bride, "Christ redeems the exiled soul in the way that medieval hostages were ransomed when captured: by paying the highest possible price."[5] The soul-bride prepares for reunion with God through a life of asceticism and virtue and, in ecstatic moments of prayer, is brought up to heaven to enjoy briefly her noble place as lady of the court.

Bernard of Clairvaux employed similar language to speak about the relationship between God and the soul. However, Mechthild takes his rather tame use of this motif much further. Her book *The Flowing Light of the Godhead* utilizes erotic language to describe her experiences of union with the Lord of the heavenly court. The following is one example of her use of these images. She writes:

> Then the bride of all delights goes to the Fairest of lovers in the secret chamber of the invisible

---

[5] Ulrike Wiethaus, "Mechthild of Magdeburg (c.1210–c.1282), The Flowing Light of the Godhead," in *Christian Spirituality: The Classics,* ed. Arthur Holder (New York: Routledge, 2010), 105.

Godhead. There she finds the bed and the abode of love prepared by God in a manner beyond what is human. Our Lord speaks:

> "Stay, Lady Soul."
> "What do you bid me, Lord?"
> "Take off your clothes."
> "Lord, what will happen to me then?"
> "Lady Soul, you are so utterly formed
>   to my nature
> That not the slightest thing can be
>   between you and me.
> Never was an angel so glorious
> That to him was granted for one hour
> What is given to you for eternity.
> And so you must cast off from you
> Both fear and shame and all external
>   virtues."[6]

As we have noted, Christians have used various metaphors to communicate knowledge of God as Beloved. In the end, what is important is not the name; it is the relationship with and knowledge of the unknown Lover that the name facilitates. Elizabeth Johnson praises the many names for God that exist in both the Christian scriptures and those of other religious traditions. The essence of God is so mysterious that the symbols we create to understand

---

[6] Frank Tobin, trans., *Mechthild of Magdeburg, The Flowing Light of the Godhead* (Mahwah, NJ: Paulist Press, 1997), 61–62.

God will never fully reveal who God is. Since God is so vast, Johnson claims, our knowledge of God is better enriched by utilizing a cornucopia of images that each reveal a facet of truth about God rather than limiting ourselves to only one, like father.[7] A greater number of images allows people with different backgrounds and experiences more opportunities to relate to the mystery we call God.

HOW IMAGES WORK

Ann Ulanov, a psychoanalyst and scholar of religion, has written about the psychological processes by which we create God images and use them to relate to God. Essentially, she writes, images of God operate through a process of projection and destruction. We need our images, or projections, to reach the God who is a mystery to us.[8] They function as bridges to the unknown. Unconsciously, we project onto God our wishes and desires. We project onto God characteristics that we wish to be true of God. (Who doesn't want a loving parent looking out for them?) Eventually, reality shatters our projections. Our projections of God as protector and supporter are challenged by the loss of a job, the death of a loved one, or the diagnosis of a serious illness. For some, such experiences end their relationship with God because their God image has been

---

[7] Elizabeth Johnson, *She Who Is: The Mystery of God in Feminist Theological Discourse* (New York: Crossroad, 1992), 120.

[8] Ann Ulanov, *Finding Space: Winnicott, God, and Psychic Reality* (Louisville, KY: Westminster John Knox Press, 2005), 110.

destroyed. Others discover that God survives the destruction of their projections.[9]

For Ulanov, projections provide a mechanism by which we can perceive unknown objects. They function as a means of perception. In this case they point to the unknown God. Though they only give us partial clues into God's nature, projections communicate something of the Divine. They are our footholds on Mount Sinai, the mysterious reality of God.

In the process of using images to relate to God, sometimes our projections get destroyed. When our images of God are destroyed, God does not cease to be. Projection and destruction are alternating phases in a process of perception that results in greater knowledge of an unknown object. Throughout this process we gradually come closer to perceiving the object as it is in itself. If we refuse to give up on God when our images get destroyed, if we are able to endure the dark night that results when we fall into the gap between our images of God and the unknown reality of God, we can experience God bridging the gap. God then moves from illusion to reality, from projection to presence.

APOPHATIC LANGUAGE

Images of God in scripture help human beings relate to the Divine. These images reveal aspects of the character of

---

[9] Ann and Barry Ulanov, *Religion and the Unconscious* (Philadelphia: Westminster Press, 1975), 40.

God whose essence is mystery, but at the same time they can also conceal God if one forgets they are only images. In addition to highlighting the diversity of images of God in scripture, Sandra Schneiders also discusses the dangers they pose. For example, a metaphor becomes problematic when it is understood literally; understanding a metaphor literally eliminates the tension between the objects being compared. It fixates on the similarity while denying the differences. For Schneiders, a metaphor taken literally is dangerous because it "paralyzes the imagination. Instead of functioning as an ever-active incentive to affective reflection on the inexhaustible mystery of the godhead, it traps the mind in a limited and therefore untrue conception of God."[10] For example, while God has many traits of a loving father, insisting on this single image masks the reality of God because it places a limit on the limitless mystery of the Divine.

Sigmund Freud (1856–1939) pushes the critique of God images even further. In *The Future of an Illusion* one of the themes that interests Freud is the psychological root of religious ideas. He asks what psychological needs religious ideas fulfill and where our images of God as Father come from. He observes that the forces of nature—whether fire, flood, earthquake, hurricane, tsunami, or cancer—mock all attempts at human control. Nature reveals our weakness and helplessness despite the moral and technical advances of civilization. To cope with this helplessness, humankind

---

[10] Schneiders, *Women and the Word*, 27.

has personified the forces of nature and converted them into gods. Freud thinks human beings learn from their earliest days that the way to influence people is to establish a relationship with them, and so later on, it is natural for them to personify everything they wish to comprehend so they can try to control it. He notes:

> Now when the child grows up and finds that he is destined to remain a child for ever, and that he can never do without protection against unknown and mighty powers, he invests these with the traits of the father-figure; he creates for himself the gods, of whom he is afraid, whom he seeks to propitiate, and to whom he nevertheless entrusts the task of protecting him.[11]

For Freud, an adult's responses to the sufferings of life are a continuation of the defensive reactions one utilized against adverse circumstances as a child. This is the reason human beings created the gods, or in this case, the heavenly Father.[12]

Consequently, although images communicate a real and relatable knowledge of God, because the knowledge they deliver is inevitably partial; what they teach us about God is limited. As Thomas Merton (1915–68) explains:

---

[11] Sigmund Freud, *The Future of an Illusion* (New York: W. W. Norton and Company, 1989), 32.

[12] Freud, *The Future of an Illusion*, 33.

"No idea of God, however pure and perfect, is adequate to express God as God really is. Our idea of God tells us more about ourselves than about God."[13]

The mystics address the tension between the way images reveal and the way they mask through two different types of language for God: *cataphatic* and *apophatic*. The images of God in scripture that began this chapter are examples of cataphatic language. Cataphatic language uses metaphors and symbols to describe what God is like. As we have noted, such images are descriptions or representations of who God is to us. They are essential because they give God a character or personality to whom people can relate. The beautiful depiction of God as a shepherd in Psalm 23 is but one example.

In contrast, apophatic language emphasizes that God is hidden, cannot be seen, and cannot be fully known. It recognizes that though descriptors such as father, mother, judge, and potter reveal something of the character of God, God is ultimately beyond any category we use to define God. This idea is not meant to undermine one's faith. It is an acknowledgment of both the incomprehensibility of the essence of God and the limits of human understanding. This aspect of God is amply attested in scripture. For example:

> Truly, you are a God who hides himself, O God of Israel, the Savior. (Isa 45:15)

---

[13] Thomas Merton, *New Seeds of Contemplation* (New York: New Directions, 1961), 15.

> For as the heavens are higher than the earth, so are my ways higher than your ways and my thoughts than your thoughts. (Isa 55:9)

> It is he alone who has immortality and dwells in unapproachable light, whom no one has ever seen or can see. (1 Tim 6:16)

> For now we see in a mirror, dimly, but then we will see face to face. Now I know only in part; then I will know fully, even as I have been fully known. (1 Cor 13:12)

Because God is beyond every name, the attitude that Meister Eckhart (1260–1328) recommends when approaching God is one of poverty of spirit. Spiritual poverty creates an openness to God by emptying the self of both the desire to fulfill its own will and to cling to a specific image of God.

Apophatic language is illustrated in the story of Moses's encounter with God on the top of Mount Sinai. In *The Life of Moses* Gregory of Nyssa (335–95 CE) offers a spiritual interpretation of Moses's experiences of God. The itinerary proceeds from light to darkness. It begins with God appearing to Moses in the flames of a burning bush and culminates with Moses entering the dark cloud at the top of the mountain. For Gregory, the spiritual journey begins with the purification of the passions. Martin Laird describes the passions as "patterns of obsession."[14]

---

[14] Martin Laird, *Into the Silent Land: A Guide to the Christian Practice of Contemplation* (New York: Oxford University Press, 2006), 51.

As human beings choose the good, cultivate the virtues, and begin to release these patterns, they make progress on the path to God. Here at the beginning of the journey, Gregory states, "Religious knowledge comes to those who receive it as light."[15] The burning bush, therefore, appears as the first theophany for Moses, not his final one. As the soul progresses on the path of moral purification, Gregory compares its growing knowledge of God to Moses's experience of God on the top of Mount Sinai. Exodus 19 and 24 state that when God called Moses to receive God's instructions for the Israelites, there was a thick cloud on the mountain. Gregory asks, "What does it mean that Moses entered the darkness and then saw God in it?"[16] Then he writes:

> For leaving behind everything that is observed, not only what sense comprehends but also what the intelligence thinks it sees, it keeps on penetrating deeper until by the intelligence's yearning for understanding it gains access to the invisible and incomprehensible, and there it sees God. This is the true knowledge of what is sought; this is the seeing that consists in not seeing, because that which is sought transcends all knowledge, being separated on all sides by incomprehensibility as by a kind of darkness.[17]

---

[15] Gregory of Nyssa, *The Life of Moses* (Mahwah, NJ: Paulist Press, 1978), 95.

[16] Gregory of Nyssa, *The Life of Moses*, 94, para. 162.

[17] Gregory of Nyssa, *The Life of Moses*, 95, para. 163.

And:

> When, therefore, Moses grew in knowledge, he declared that he had seen God in the darkness, that is, that he had then come to know that what is divine is beyond all knowledge and comprehension.[18]

For Gregory, God is beyond all knowledge and comprehension. God transcends every image or description. God is like a loving human father, but in reality God is much more than this or any other image can describe. At the end of all of our attempts to understand God, the essence of God is ineffable. This is represented by the darkness at the top of the mountain.

SINAI AND TABOR

Belden Lane explores the significance of geography and place in the history of spirituality, especially how imagery of perilous places like mountains and deserts is used to communicate the unknowable God of the apophatic way.[19] He claims that scripture uses the mountains of Sinai and Tabor to symbolize apophatic and cataphatic language about God. In first-person accounts of his travels Lane describes Sinai as a desolate place akin to the surface of the moon:"There is almost no vegetation . . . only Nubian

---

[18] Gregory of Nyssa, *The Life of Moses*, 95, para. 164.

[19] Belden Lane, *The Solace of Fierce Landscapes: Exploring Desert and Mountain Spirituality* (New York: Oxford University Press, 1998).

sandstone and stark, red and black granite."[20] Mount Tabor in Galilee, which Christians claim to be the site of Jesus's transfiguration, "by contrast, offers a landscape of accessible and gentle beauty. Like a wet, green breast rising out of the plains of Jezreel, it is bathed in light, covered with woodland trees and wildflowers."[21] In addition to the sharp contrast in appearance, ascending Sinai is a much more formidable task. The summit of Mount Sinai is 7497 feet, compared to only 1730 feet for Mount Tabor. There is even a road to the top of Mount Tabor, where there is a Franciscan church.

The physical differences between these mountains illustrate the two distinct theological approaches. The desolate landscape of Mount Sinai, on the one hand, represents the mysterious, ineffable character of God, which resists every attempt of human language to name and define it. The God of Sinai refuses to be limited and strikes fear in the hearts of those who would try to approach. Mount Tabor, on the other hand, is much more welcoming and accessible; it is the place where Jesus was bathed in light and glorified by the Father before the disciples. On Mount Tabor, instead of remaining concealed, God clearly and dramatically advertises, "I am here!"

COMPLEMENTARY PATHS

Though the distinction between apophatic and cataphatic language helps to clarify the two main verbal strategies

---

[20] Lane, *The Solace of Fierce Landscapes*, 113.

[21] Lane, *The Solace of Fierce Landscapes*, 124–25.

mystics use to describe the mysterious reality of God, it can give the impression that they are completely separate paths with opposing spiritualities.[22] The apophatic and cataphatic, however, are not routes that can be traveled in isolation from one another. As we noted earlier, scripture uses various names for God and declares that God is hidden in mystery. Therefore, there is a dialectical tension between these two modes of discourse. They require each other. Thomas Merton states:

> We must affirm and deny at the same time. One cannot go without the other. If we go on affirming, without denying, we end up by affirming that we have delimited the Being of God in our concepts. If we go on denying without affirming, we end up by denying that our concepts can tell the truth about Him in any sense whatever.[23]

Or, as Lane writes, "Language about God is as impossible as it is necessary."[24]

An illustration of the interconnectedness between these two modes of discourse is that, despite its bias toward iconoclasm, apophatic language often makes use of im-

---

[22] The term *verbal strategies* comes from the work of Bernard Mc-Ginn. See Bernard McGinn, "General Introduction," in *Foundations of Mysticism: Origins to the Fifth Century* (New York: Crossroad, 1991), xvii.

[23] Thomas Merton, *Ascent to Truth* (New York: Harcourt Brace, 1951), 94.

[24] Lane, *The Solace of Fierce Landscapes*, 104.

ages. In the end, what characterizes apophatic discourse
is not a denial of images; it is what those images seek to
convey. Cataphatic discourse uses human language to
bring the mystery of God into greater focus. Apophatic
discourse uses images from threatening places—mountain,
cloud, wilderness, desert, cave, exile, and even the belly of
a fish—because images such as these, instead of providing
clear access to God, reveal the limits of language and the
ego's attempts to control reality. Lane writes:

> The apophatic tradition, despite its distrust of all
> images about God, makes an exception in using the
> imagery of threatening places as a way of challenging
> the ego and leaving one at a loss for words. If we
> cannot know God's essence, we can stand in God's
> place—on the high mountain, in the lonely desert,
> at the point where terror gives way to wonder. Only
> there do we enter the abandonment, the *agnosia*, that
> is finally necessary for meeting God.[25]

In this chapter we explored the language used in
scripture and the contemplative tradition to describe the
character of God. In the next chapter we explore the
mystic's understanding of the human person. How are we
related to God?

---

[25] Lane, *The Solace of Fierce Landscapes*, 65.

4

A Contemplative Anthropology

Just as Origen distinguishes between the letter and spirit of scripture, he—and many Christian mystics—also believes human beings are composed of two parts, an inner and an outer.[1] We can observe this phenomenon as we engage in different levels of meaning in our daily pursuits. Some of these activities are necessary, such as obtaining proper food, clothing, shelter, and living in community. Others are simply diversions, such as obsessions with social media, news, sports, gaming, or shopping. We might also devote time to activities that are close to our deepest sense of who we are—or want to be—such as artistic pursuits, volunteer work, or being consciously present to our families. Finally, for someone on a spiritual path, nourishing one's most basic sense of self and its relationship to the Divine can include devoting intentional time to being in nature or immersing oneself in quiet, solitude, reading, and contemplation.

[1] Origen, "Commentary on the Song of Songs," in *The Essential Writings of Christian Mysticism*, ed. Bernard McGinn (New York: Modern Library, 2006), 8.

Some, however, are critical of making a distinction between an inner and outer self. John Swinton notes that the idea of human beings possessing an inner life is a useful metaphor, but in reality "the inner life is not a thing, a space or a place. It is a linguistic device designed to enable us to make sense of our subjectivity and awareness."[2] Swinton believes that because it has been used so often over the centuries, the concept of the inner life has been reified. He is concerned that the metaphor has been assumed to be real. This is dangerous because it elevates the inner life over the outer life by assuming that our deepest spiritual knowledge is cultivated through introspection rather than action.[3] In reality, our inner lives are interconnected with our outer lives of action, and with the outer lives of others. Therefore, the concept of the inner life is an impoverishment of our understanding of the self because it prioritizes individual self-reflection over self-knowledge gained through action and relationships.

. David Perrin is also critical of spiritual writing that encourages a search for one's inner or true self. He notes that such a search is complicated by the fact that the self is both stable and unstable. There is, on the one hand, a "stable and identifiable 'I' that possesses learned beliefs, attitudes, and opinions that situate the individual in a

---

[2] John Swinton, "Interiority and Christian Spirituality: Why Our Inner Lives Are Not Quite as Inner as We Might Like to Think," in *Sacrality and Materiality: Locating Intersections*, ed. Rebecca Giselbrecht and Ralph Kunz (Göttingen: Vandenhoek and Ruprecht, 2016), 159.

[3] Swinton, "Interiority and Christian Spirituality," 160.

personal existence."[4] On the other hand, "the self is continually being constructed and is susceptible to change. New experiences shape the self in new ways."[5] The self is not a preformed entity waiting to be uncovered; it cannot be isolated with absolute certainty. It is elusive and always subject to change and development. The self, though it has an identifiable center, is a mystery and a paradox that is always in flux as it undergoes new experiences.

Martin Laird suggests that the "true self" versus "false self" distinction is dualistic. He finds the external or false self to be especially problematic. The false self is not a distinct part of the self that is opposed to the true or inner self but an illusion that makes us think we are separate from God. For Laird, we are not fundamentally separate from God; we only seem to be. The problem with contrasting a false self with a true self is that setting up such a dichotomy implies that the false or external self is real, when, in fact, it is only an illusion sustained by our mental clutter.[6]

---

[4] David Perrin, *Studying Christian Spirituality* (New York: Routledge, 2007), 126.

[5] Perrin, *Studying Christian Spirituality*.

[6] Martin Laird, *An Ocean of Light: Contemplation, Transformation, and Liberation* (New York: Oxford University Press, 2019), 55. We explore Laird's teaching on contemplation in Chapter 6. Bernadette Roberts (1931–2017) goes even farther than Laird. She claims that at the end of the mystical journey, there is no self at all. Bernadette Roberts, *The Path to No-Self: Life at the Center* (Albany: State University of New York Press, 1991).

The issues Swinton, Perrin, and Laird raise are genuine. As we move forward, their critiques will be an important check on the material presented. As I advance a picture of the human person composed of an inner and outer self, it will be important to remember that the cultivation of the inner self does not come at the exclusion of the outer life of action and relationships, that any understanding of the self is elusive because the self is always changing, and that the false self is ultimately only an illusion. Despite these concerns, the metaphor of the inner and outer self is a useful one. This chapter explores this distinction because it helps us understand who we are and how we are related to God. We begin with how scripture describes the inner self.

THE INNER SELF

Genesis states that God created human beings in the image and likeness of God (1:26). The text does not explain what this means, but being created in God's image suggests that we are related to God in an intrinsic fashion. Bernard McGinn explains that in traditional monastic theology, "to be an image of anything means to participate in it, that is, to receive reality from it, but also to be distinguishable from it in some way."[7] To be created in the image of God means that something in our essence is

---

[7] Bernard McGinn, "Living the Trinity: William of St. Thierry," in *Early Christian Mystics: The Divine Vision of Spiritual Masters* (New York: Crossroad, 2003), 235.

fundamentally connected to God. This grants us a dignity and a potential for relationship that are inherent in what it means to be human.

If the concept of image implies being connected with God in the deepest part of our being, likeness is the degree to which we realize this potential to be in relationship with God. Realizing this potential, however, is not guaranteed because it is impaired by sin.[8] In addition to being about relationship, likeness is also about resemblance. Likeness represents the extent to which we reflect the light of God. It indicates the degree to which we manifest the beauty of the image in which we have been created.[9] The Gospel of Luke provides an illustration of the relationship between image and likeness, "The disciple is not above the teacher, but everyone who is fully qualified will be like the teacher" (6:40). The mystical life is a journey in which we seek to grow in likeness to that of our teacher, Jesus Christ, who is also our deepest self.

Scripture talks about the inner self, or the image of God within us, in various ways. For example, Paul writes about an inner self in conflict with an outer self that is conformed to the ways of the world, "For I delight in the law of God in my inmost self, but I see in my members

---

[8] As we will see in Chapter 6, for those on a spiritual path, the "sin" that most hinders relationship with God is our preoccupation with our thoughts and not with reality as it is present before us.

[9] Jean Daniélou, *From Glory to Glory: Texts from Gregory of Nyssa's Mystical Writings*, ed. and trans. Herbert Musurillo (Crestwood, NY: St. Vladimir's Seminary Press, 1995), 113–14.

another law at war with the law of my mind, making me captive to the law of sin that dwells in my members" (Rom 7:22–23). Jesus says, "The kingdom of God is within you" (Lk 17:21, KJV). Although not in the canon, the slight differences between the Gospel of Thomas and the canonical Gospels can provide a fresh perspective on texts like this one from the Gospel of Luke.[10] In the Gospel of Thomas, Jesus says:

> If those who seek to attract you say to you: "See, the Kingdom is in heaven!" then the birds of heaven will be there before you. If they say to you: "It is in the sea!" then the fish will be there before you. But the kingdom is within you and it is outside of you! When you know yourselves, then you will be known, and you will know that it is you who are the sons of the living Father. But if you do not know yourselves, then you will be in a state of poverty, and it is you [who] will be the poverty! (Saying 3)

The most prominent metaphor used in scripture to describe the inner self is the heart, which stands in contrast to the superficial or surface-level dimensions of the human person (cf. 1 Sam 16:7). The heart is not the source of our transitory feelings; it designates our deepest center. It is the fountain from which our most fundamental thoughts and

---

[10] Note that the Gospel of Thomas does not present the story of Jesus's life; it simply recounts 114 sayings of Jesus.

moral decisions flow (cf. 1 Cor 4:5; Heb 4:12). It is also the site of divine encounter, the place within that God illuminates and Christ indwells (cf. Rom 5:5; Eph 3:17; 2 Cor 4:6).[11] John McGuckin describes it as "a place of epiphany."[12]

The theme of the heart as the deepest center of a person is particularly prominent in Orthodox spirituality. For example, Eastern Christian writers interpret Psalm 64:6 to mean that the heart contains great depths, and its deepest part is the part of the human being that is in contact with God. The fourth-century Syrian monk known as Pseudo-Macarius describes Christ's presence in the heart:

> There are, therefore, infinite depths to the human heart. There are found reception rooms, bedrooms, doors and antechambers, many offices and exits. . . . There takes place upright business as well as the contrary. . . . The heart is the palace of Christ and it abounds with every kind of impurity and with great crowds of evil spirits. It is, therefore, necessary to repair and rebuild it; its storerooms and bedrooms must be cleaned up. For Christ the King with his angels and spirits is coming there so that he may find

---

[11] John McGuckin, "The Prayer of the Heart in Patristic and Early Byzantine Tradition," in *Illumined in the Spirit: Studies in Orthodox Spirituality* (Yonkers, NY: St. Vladimir's Seminary Press, 2017), 62–63.

[12] John McGuckin, *Standing in God's Holy Fire: The Byzantine Tradition* (Maryknoll, NY: Orbis Books, 2001), 74.

his rest, he may live and move about freely and set up his kingdom.[13]

For Pseudo-Macarius, Christ is present in the heart; also present are sources of "impurity." Therefore, vigilance is necessary to guard the heart, for only "the pure in heart will see God" (Mt 5:8).[14] Similarly, Thomas Merton depicts the heart as "the deepest psychological ground of one's personality, the inner sanctuary where self-awareness goes beyond analytical reflection and opens out into metaphysical and theological confrontation with the Abyss of the unknown yet present—one who is 'more intimate to us than we are to ourselves.'"[15]

Along with scripture, the great Christian mystics also address the inner self. Echoing Colossians, "Your life is hidden with Christ in God" (3:3), each of the following writers speak of this inner self and its innate connection to God: "You were more inward than my inmost part" (Augustine);[16] "You were within and I was in the external world and sought you there" (Augustine);[17] "He is your being but you are not his" (*The Book of Privy Counseling,*

---

[13] Pseudo-Macarius, *The Fifty Spiritual Homilies and the Great Letter*, trans. George Maloney (Mahwah, NJ: Paulist Press, 1992), 120.

[14] We explore the practice of watchfulness or interior vigilance in Chapter 6.

[15] Thomas Merton, *Contemplative Prayer* (New York: Image Books, 1996), 33.

[16] Augustine, *Confessions*, trans. Henry Chadwick (New York: Oxford University Press, 1991), 43.

[17] Augustine, *Confessions*, 201.

fourteenth century);[18] "Our soul is created to be God's
dwelling place, and the dwelling of our soul is God, who is
uncreated" (Julian of Norwich, 1342–1416);[19] "The soul's
center is God" (John of the Cross, 1542–91);[20] "My 'I' is
hidden for me (and for others); it is on the side of God,
it is in God, it is God. To be proud is to forget that one
is God" (Simone Weil, 1909–43).[21] And Thomas Merton
writes:

> At the center of our being is a point of nothingness
> which is untouched by sin and by illusion, a point of
> pure truth, a point or spark which belongs entirely
> to God, which is never at our disposal, from which
> God disposes of our lives, which is inaccessible to
> the fantasies of our own mind or the brutalities of
> our own will. This little point of nothingness and of
> absolute poverty is the pure glory of God in us. It is
> so to speak His name written in us, as our poverty, as
> our indigence, as our dependence, as our sonship. It is
> like a pure diamond, blazing with the invisible light
> of heaven. It is in everybody, and if we could see it

---

[18] *The Cloud of Unknowing and the Book of Privy Counseling*, trans.
William Johnston (New York: Image Books, 1973), 150.

[19] Julian of Norwich, *Showings* (Mahwah, NJ: Paulist Press, 1978),
285.

[20] John of the Cross, *The Living Flame of Love*, I, 12, in *The Collected
Works of St. John of the Cross*, trans. Kieran Kavanaugh and Otilio Ro-
driguez (Washington, DC: Institute of Carmelite Studies, 1979), 583.

[21] Simone Weil, *Gravity and Grace* (Lincoln: University of Nebraska
Press, 1997), 85.

we would see these billions of points of light coming together in the face and blaze of a sun that would make all the darkness and cruelty of life vanish completely. . . . I have no program for this seeing. It is only given. But the gate of heaven is everywhere.[22]

For the mystics, Jacob voices the fundamental problem with human existence when he exclaims, "Surely the Lord is in this place—and I did not know it!" (Gen 28:16). For these writers we are not separate from God. From the perspective of our everyday dualistic consciousness, it only appears that we are. The distinctions we make in daily life between subject and object don't tell the full story of the relationship between God and ourselves (and ourselves and everything else). Though the normal contrast we make between the "me" and the "not-me" may accurately describe external differences between objects, for the mystics this distinction is only true on the surface. It's not the full truth about reality. Yet, this unitive vision is not how we usually perceive the world. A series of attitudes that are outlined below cloud our minds and prevent us from sensing our innate connection to God.

THE OUTER SELF

Gregory of Nyssa uses two suggestive images, the mirror and the seal, to describe the relationship between the

---

[22] Thomas Merton, *Conjectures of a Guilty Bystander* (New York: Image Books, 1989), 158.

inner self and God. First, because of free will, human nature can manifest either virtue or vice.[23] Our nature, therefore, is like a mirror that reflects whatever lies in front of it. The task of the spiritual life is to reflect the light of Christ. The goal is to let the soul's original beauty, which was created in the image of God, shine forth. The problem is that we let dirt (or sin) tarnish the surface of our mirrors. Our various cravings and obsessive thoughts occupy our minds and obscure the image of God hidden underneath. Once this rust or dirt is removed, the image of God will again shine out from within us[24] (cf. Sir 12:11; 2 Cor 3:18). Second, when we were created, God imprinted God's image upon us like a seal that makes an impression on wax[25] (2 Cor 1:22; Eph 1:13). Our sin hides this impression with a "vicious" coating. When this happens, Gregory says, "You must then wash away, by a life of virtue, the dirt that has come to cling to your heart like plaster, and then your divine beauty will once again shine forth."[26]

In a great example of the spiritual interpretation of scripture, Origen interprets the coin in the parable of the lost coin (Lk 15:8–10) as the image of God in the soul:

> And that woman who had lost a drachma did not find it on the outside, but in her house, after "she lit

---

[23] Daniélou, *From Glory to Glory*, 170–71.

[24] Daniélou, *From Glory to Glory*, 113–14.

[25] Daniélou, *From Glory to Glory*, 101.

[26] Daniélou, *From Glory to Glory*.

a lamp and cleaned her house" from dirt and filth which the sloth and dullness of a long time had heaped up, and then she found the drachma. And, therefore, if you should light a lamp, if you should devote your attention to the illumination of the Holy Spirit and "see the light in his light," you will discover a drachma within you. For the image of the heavenly king has been placed within you.

For when God made man in the beginning, "he made him according to his own image and likeness"; and he did not place this image on the outside, but within him. This image could not be seen in you as long as your house was dirty with filth and filled with rubbish . . . [but now] having been cleansed from that whole earthly mass and weight by the Word of God, make the "image of the heavenly" shine brightly in you. . . . The son of God is the painter of this image. And because he is such a great painter his image can be obscured by negligence; it cannot be destroyed by malice. For the image of God always remains, even if you yourself draw "the image of the earthly" over it in yourself.[27]

Our goal should be to grow into the likeness of Christ, but we often fail to reflect God's light. If a clean and

---

[27] Origen, *Homilies on Genesis and Exodus*, trans. Ronald Heine (Washington, DC: Catholic University of America Press, 1982), 191–93.

polished mirror symbolizes our inner self, a tarnished one represents our outer self. Augustine's classic definition of original sin, that human beings are "curved in" on themselves, captures well the self-preoccupation that isolates us from God and our neighbor. One way this being "curved in" affects the spiritual life today is that we are constantly wrapped up in our heads. Matthew 6:25–34 addresses some of the anxious thoughts that rattle around inside our minds. In contrast, Matthew 5:8 says, "Blessed are the pure in heart, for they will see God." Instead of something like *virtuous* or *unstained,* Cynthia Bourgeault claims *purity* in this verse means singleness— or focus—of mind and heart.[28] From a contemplative perspective the mirror of our inner self does not reflect God's light when we are uncollected, when our attention and energies are scattered among a variety of thoughts and preferences (cf. Jas 4:8). Novelist David Foster Wallace (1962–2008) described this condition when he stated, "It is extremely difficult to stay alert and attentive, instead of getting hypnotized by the constant monologue inside your own head."[29] Similarly, Orthodox scholar Maximos Constas spiritually interprets the "wealth" the prodigal son squanders in a distant country as his focus and at-

---

[28] Cynthia Bourgeault, *The Wisdom Jesus* (Boulder, CO: Shambhala, 2008), 45–46.

[29] David Foster Wallace, "This Is Water," 2005 commencement speech, Kenyon College.

tention.[30] Read this way, the "home" the prodigal returns to is the present moment.[31]

THOMAS MERTON'S TRUE AND FALSE SELF

Thomas Merton presents a psychological model of these two aspects of the human person through his metaphor of the true and false self: "There is in us a native and ongoing contest between our deepest ground and a more shallow identity which seems more familiar to us, which we are more ready to accept as 'ourselves,' and which we prefer to this inner and transcendental ground of freedom."[32] For Merton, the false self is the exterior, surface, or superficial self, the self that finds its identity in how it differs from other selves. The false self is the aspect of the self that is guided by the ego.

The development of a strong, sturdy ego is an important task throughout life as new psychological capacities, such as resilience, adaptability, or self-efficacy, are needed. In the tradition of depth psychology, infants identify with the unconscious because a caregiver, at first, responds

---

[30] Maximos Constas, "Attend to Thyself (Deut 15:9): Attentiveness and Digital Culture," International Conference on Digital Media and Orthodox Pastoral Care, Athens, May, 7–9, 2015. https://hcgost. academia.edu/FrMaximosConstas.

[31] Brian Pierce, *We Walk the Path Together* (Maryknoll, NY: Orbis Books, 2005), 23.

[32] Thomas Merton, *Opening the Bible* (Collegeville, MN: Liturgical Press, 1986), 76.

seamlessly to their needs. Eventually, children feel the need to differentiate between the unconscious and those around them—such as parents—who quickly provided the necessities of life early on. This differentiation occurs through acts of the will. For children, this stage is apparent when their response always seems to be "no" and possessions are marked off as "mine." Through these and similar actions, the ego strives to achieve a secure hold on identity by defining who one is and what one wants.

Without a strong, sturdy ego, a person wouldn't be able to act confidently or cope with adversity. One's resilience in the face of hardship would be low. The danger for the spiritual life, here, is that people can spend their entire life at the stage of the ego. They may never move beyond forming their identity by how they differ from others.

Thomas Merton loved the question, "Who am I?" The true or inner self, however, is not easily identified. We can't see it in a selfie or in our retirement account balance. The inner self is difficult to pin down because it is shy and fundamentally unknown (cf. Jer 17:9–10; Isa 29:13). On this aspect of the true self Merton writes:

> The inner self is precisely that self which cannot be tricked or manipulated by anyone, even by the devil. He is like a very wild animal that never appears at all whenever an alien presence is at hand, and comes out only when all is perfectly peaceful, in silence, when he is untroubled and alone. He cannot be lured by

anyone or anything, because he responds to no lure except that of divine freedom.[33]

The true self is difficult to describe because it only knows itself in relationship with God. Merton elaborates on this:

Since we are made in the image and likeness of God, there is no other way for us to find out who we are than by finding, in ourselves the divine image.[34]

Self-realization in this true religious sense is then less an awareness of ourselves than an awareness of the God to whom we are drawn in the depths of our own being. We become real, and experience our actuality, not when we pause to reflect upon our own self as an isolated entity, but rather when, transcending ourselves and passing beyond reflection, we center our whole soul upon the God Who is our life. That is to say we fully "realize" ourselves when we cease to be conscious of ourselves in separateness and know nothing but the one God Who is above all knowledge.[35]

---

[33] Lawrence Cunningham, ed., *Thomas Merton: Spiritual Master, The Essential Writings* (Mahwah, NJ: Paulist Press, 1992), 297.

[34] Thomas Merton, *The New Man* (New York: Farrar, Straus, and Giroux, 1999), 120.

[35] Merton, *The New Man*, 122.

In another place he states:

> In Christianity the inner self is simply a stepping stone to an awareness of God. Man is the image of God, and his inner self is a kind of mirror in which God not only sees Himself, but reveals Himself to the "mirror" in which He is reflected. Thus, through the dark, transparent mystery of our own inner being we can, as it were, see God "through a glass." All this is of course pure metaphor. It is a way of saying that our being somehow communicates directly with the Being of God, Who is "in us." If we enter into ourselves, find our true self, and then pass "beyond" the inner "I," we sail forth into the immense darkness in which we confront the "I AM" of the Almighty.[36]

Thus, for Merton, to know our true self is not to uncover some unchanging core of the personality through self-reflection. Essentially, to know the true self is to stop identifying with our external identity and, through the practice of contemplation, receive the awareness that God is our deepest center. Therefore, the true self is not a thing; it is an experience. For Merton, it is "in prayer, we discover what we already have. You start where you are and you deepen what you already have and you realize you are already there. We already have everything, but we don't know it and we don't experience it. Everything has been

---

[36] Cunningham, *Thomas Merton: Spiritual Master*, 302.

given to us in Christ. All we need is to experience what we already possess."[37]

Unlike the true self, the false or external self is more easily observable, if we know where to look. We don't enter the world knowing who we are. Beyond our relationship with God, there are many other influences that can define us. As we noted above, establishing a strong ego is essential to functioning effectively in the world, and the ego defines itself by contrasting itself with others. Thomas Merton, however, describes the ego as a false or superficial self. The false self provides a way to stand out from the crowd. It is a mask that shows others our uniqueness. Merton insists that, while we invest enormous amounts of time and energy on the false self, it can never be our true identity because it is only concerned with external appearances. It can't penetrate the surface to tell us who we really are. He describes the false self this way:

> People who know nothing of God and whose lives are centered on themselves, imagine that they can only find themselves by asserting their own desires and ambitions and appetites in a struggle with the rest of the world. They try to become real by imposing themselves on other people, by appropriating for themselves some share of the limited supply of created goods and thus emphasizing the difference

---

[37] David Steindl-Rast, "Man of Prayer," in *Thomas Merton/Monk: A Monastic Tribute*, ed. Patrick Hart (London: Sheed and Ward, 1974), 80.

between themselves and the other men who have less than they, or nothing at all. They can only conceive one way of becoming real: cutting themselves off from other people and building a barrier of contrast and distinction between themselves and other men.[38]

The false self, he explains, focuses on differences between itself and others:

I have what you have not. I am what you are not. I have taken what you have failed to take and I have seized what you could never get. Therefore you suffer and I am happy, you are despised and I am praised, you die and I live; you are nothing and I am something, and I am all the more something because you are nothing. And thus I spend my life admiring the distance between you and me.[39]

The false self finds its identity by defining how it differs from others. For Merton, the false self likes to tell itself: "I am not like other men."[40]

When I introduce the external self to students, I suggest that the ego fundamentally has an inferiority complex.

---

[38] Thomas Merton, *New Seeds of Contemplation* (New York: New Directions, 1961), 47.

[39] Merton, *New Seeds of Contemplation*, 48.

[40] Merton, *New Seeds of Contemplation*, 50.

Because the ego feels inadequate, it creates the false self to prop itself up. The external self is the mask we wear to impress others, and it likes attention. This false self is the image or facade we show the world to generate the best possible impression. It is the part of us that pulls out our selfie stick to take the most flattering pictures possible. It is the carefully edited version of ourselves we show others on Instagram or Facebook, the part of us that gets a psychological lift when we receive lots of "likes." The false self is an identity we form to create a stronger sense of self. It is the makeup we put on to show those around us that we are attractive, smart, funny, and cool under pressure. To say that we have an external self means that when we are in public, we are always acting—always, to some degree, playing a role.

Basil Pennington (1931–2005) writes that the false self "is made up of what I have, what I do, and what others think of me."[41] Much of our self-identity is based on our work. We want to be able to take pride in what we do. We want to be able to tell people that we're a doctor or a banker, own our own business, or work for a prestigious company. We also aspire to drive a luxury car and live in a hip neighborhood because of the status they confer. These are things we can declare with pride if anyone asks where we work, what we drive, or where we live.

---

[41] M. Basil Pennington, *True Self/False Self: Unmasking the Spirit Within* (New York: Crossroad, 2000), 31.

In other words, the external self is the image we carry of ourselves that (we think) distinguishes us from others. It is the identity we form about ourselves that (we think) makes us special. It can include the fact that you think you are special because you are fit or you are funny, that we have great hair or excellent taste in music, that we have an awesome apartment or a great-fitting suit. In one of my favorite Merton passages, he takes aim (with a bit of hyperbole) at perhaps the most fundamental desire of the false self:

> A few years ago a man who was compiling a book entitled *Success* wrote and asked me to contribute a statement on how I got to be a success. I replied indignantly that I was not able to consider myself a success in any terms that had a meaning to me. I swore I had spent my life strenuously avoiding success. If it so happened that I had once written a best seller, this was a pure accident, due to inattention and naivete, and I would take very good care never to do the same again. If I had a message to my contemporaries, I said, it was surely this: Be anything you like, be madmen, drunks, and bastards of every shape and form, but at all costs avoid one thing: success.[42]

Several years ago a student remarked with a note of frustration: "All these readings are telling us we're fake."

---

[42] Cunningham, *Thomas Merton: Spiritual Master,* 364–65.

Therefore, let me clarify what the false self *doesn't* mean.
Despite the negative connotations associated with terms
like *external* and *superficial,* the false self is not an inherently
negative thing. It is simply a stage we all go through as we
come to understand who we are in relation to everyone
else. Richard Rohr describes the provisional nature of the
false self this way:

> Your False Self, which we might also call your "small
> self," is your launching pad: your body image, your job,
> your education, your clothes, your money, your car,
> your sexual identity, your success, and so on. These are
> the trappings of ego that we all use to get us through
> an ordinary day. They are a nice enough platform to
> stand on, but they are largely a projection of our self-
> image and our attachment to it. When you are able to
> move beyond your False Self—at the right time and
> in the right way—*it will feel precisely as if you have lost
> nothing.* In fact, it will feel like freedom and liberation.
> When you are connected to the Whole, you no longer
> need to protect or defend the mere part. You are now
> connected to something inexhaustible.[43]

For Merton, the external self is an identity we construct
that presents the face we want to display to the world. It is
a mask that delineates how we differ from others. Though

---

[43] Richard Rohr, *Immortal Diamond: The Search for Our True Self* (San
Francisco: Jossey-Bass, 2013), 28.

we can be extremely attached to it, it is just a disguise. It is not real. Merton refers to it as "unsubstantial."[44] Martin Laird says the false self is an illusion that makes us think we are separate from God and other people. In the end Thomas Merton thinks the external self deserves mercy.[45] To have mercy on the false self means to accept it as a provisional step on the journey to understanding who we really are. It suggests that we should have compassion on it, because developmentally we must cultivate a secure ego identity before we can let it go and because "the mask that each man wears may well be a disguise not only for the man's inner self but for God, wandering as a pilgrim and exile in His own creation."[46]

THREE MORE CHARACTERISTICS
OF THE FALSE SELF

Merton's concept of the false self is a suggestive one. He addressed it in many of his writings but did not develop it at length. Building on his idea, resources in scripture and the contemplative tradition allow us to advance three more characteristics of the false self. The first is that we are constantly judging. (Jesus talks about how judging blinds us in Matthew 7:1–5.) In life, our minds are continually labeling, categorizing, and ranking things. Just as we unconsciously

---

[44] Merton, *New Seeds of Contemplation*, 295.

[45] Merton, *New Seeds of Contemplation*, 295.

[46] Merton, *New Seeds of Contemplation*, 296.

take thousands of breaths each day, our minds involuntarily generate preferences; our fundamental reaction to something is usually whether we like it or not. The danger in this ceaseless generation of mental judgments is that it traps us in our heads and separates us from other people. Robert Wright argues that the mental labels we affix on things actually create the boundaries we perceive between the "me" and the "not-me."[47] The distinctions we draw between "self" and "other" prevent us from seeing what we have in common with other people. Merton notes that the desert fathers and mothers of the fourth century were so sensitive to the corrosive effects of judgmental thoughts that they refused to criticize or condemn others, even when presented with evidence against the accused.[48] In a similar spirit of detachment from one's will the poet Angelus Silesius (1624–77) writes:

> I wonder what to do! To me it's all the same:
> Place, no-place, eternity, night, day, and joy
> and pain.[49]

A second and related characteristic of the false self is that in the process of making judgments about everything

---

[47] Robert Wright, *Why Buddhism Is True: The Science and Philosophy of Meditation and Enlightenment* (New York: Simon and Schuster, 2017), 151–52, 207–13, 229.

[48] Patrick O'Connell, ed., *Thomas Merton: Selected Essays* (Maryknoll, NY: Orbis Books, 2013), 318.

[49] Maria Shrady, trans., *Angelus Silesius: The Cherubinic Wanderer* (Mahwah, NJ: Paulist Press, 1986), 46.

that comes before us, we compare ourselves to other people. Scripture specifically warns us against this (cf. 2 Cor 10:12; Lk 9:46; Lk 22:24). Evagrius Ponticus (345–99) writes, "If your spirit still looks around at the time of prayer, then it does not truly pray."[50] Similar to the habit of judging in general, this practice keeps us focused on the exterior surface of life and makes it difficult to see the ways in which we are connected to others. This comparison occurs, for example, when we scan social media and see all the fabulous things our friends are doing that we aren't. Another way such comparison manifests itself is when our first thought after hearing about an achievement of a colleague is about ourselves. We ask, "When is something good going to happen to *me*? When am *I* going to get a new job or a promotion?" On comparing ourselves with others, Merton offers the following thoughts:

> As soon as you begin to take yourself seriously and imagine that your virtues are important because they are yours, you become the prisoner of your own vanity and even your best works will blind and deceive you. Then, in order to defend yourself, you will begin to see sins and faults everywhere in the actions of other men. And the more unreasonable importance you attach to yourself and to your own

---

[50] Evagrius Ponticus, *The Praktikos and Chapters on Prayer*, ed. John Eudes Bamberger (Collegeville, MN: Cistercian Publications, 1972), 61–62, no. 43 (translation slightly altered).

works, the more you will tend to build up your own idea of yourself by condemning other people. Sometimes virtuous men are also bitter and unhappy, because they have unconsciously come to believe that all their happiness depends on their being more virtuous than others.[51]

Engaging in this type of comparison leads to spiritual pride, the belief that our virtues make us better than others. An example of this in scripture is the parable of the Pharisee and the tax collector in Luke 18. When the Pharisee noticed the tax collector in the Temple, all he saw was what was different between the two of them. Because of his pride, he was blind to the things they had in common. Furthermore, telling others about our virtuous practices is also a subtle form of spiritual pride. On this, the desert monks write:

> One day in the Vale of the Hermitages, when a feast was being celebrated, the brethren were eating together in their place of assembly. A certain brother said to those who were serving at table, "I won't eat anything cooked, just a little salt on my bread."
>
> The one who was serving at table called to another brother and said in the presence of the whole gathering, "This brother is not eating anything cooked. Bring him just a little salt."

---

[51] Merton, *New Seeds of Contemplation*, 57–58.

> Then one of the elders rose and said to the broth-
> er who has asked for salt, "It would have been better
> for you today to eat meat alone in your cell, rather
> than to publish what you are doing to so many of
> the brethren."[52]

A third characteristic of the false self is the desire to be
in control. Richard Rohr defines suffering as "whenever
you are not in control."[53] One of the ways we try to stay
in control of our lives is by worrying. We believe that if
we can understand every facet of a problem from every
possible angle, this will somehow mitigate the frustrating
situation in which we find ourselves. Another tactic to
maintain the illusion of control is keeping the things we
have to do in the front of our mind, believing that this
will help us get these things accomplished more effectively when we actually have time to work on them. In
contrast to such strategies, Jesus says, "Do not worry" (Mt
6:25–34). When Jesus tells his audience not to worry, he
means that we should surrender our desired outcome and
yield to God's will in every situation. When we learn to
stop insisting that things work out the way we want them
to, we find that we receive what we need without having
to go through the stress of worrying about it. For Meister

[52] Olivier Clément, *The Roots of Christian Mysticism: Texts from the Patristic Era with Commentary*, 2nd ed. (New York: New City Press, 1993), 158.

[53] Richard Rohr, *Things Hidden: Scripture as Spirituality* (Cincinnati, OH: St. Anthony Messenger Press, 2007), 25.

Eckhart, for example, whatever happens is God's will, so we should accept the things that happen to us rather than internally resist what life brings. He writes:

> When it falls to some people to suffer or to do something, they say, "If only I knew it was God's will, I would gladly endure it or do it!" Dear God! that is a strange question for a sick man to ask, whether it is God's will that he should be sick. He ought to realize that if he is sick, it *must* be God's will. It is just the same with other things. And so a man should accept from God, purely and simply, whatever happens to him.[54]

Therefore, Eckhart doesn't recommend petitionary prayer; he mockingly calls people who pray for things they want "donkeys."[55] He declares, "If a man had no more to do with God than to be thankful, that would suffice."[56] The "thank you" confirms that we are in alignment with whatever arises, that we have emptied ourselves of the desire for things to align with our preferences. Thus, to pray rightly,

---

[54] Meister Eckhart, *The Complete Mystical Works of Meister Eckhart,* trans. Maurice O'C Walshe (New York: Crossroad, 2010), 290.

[55] Bernard McGinn, *The Mystical Thought of Meister Eckhart: The Man from Whom God Hid Nothing* (New York: Crossroad, 2001), 131; Louis Dupre and James Wiseman, eds., "Meister Eckhart (c. 1260–c. 1329)," in *Light from Light: An Anthology of Christian Mysticism*, 2nd ed. (Mahwah, NJ: Paulist Press, 2001), 167.

[56] Eckhart, *The Complete Mystical Works*, 173.

for Eckhart, is to request, not something for ourselves, but as Jesus taught in the Our Father, "Thy will be done." When we learn to pray this way, Eckhart says, we always get what we ask for.[57]

KENOSIS

If the human person is made up of a true and a false self, what, then, is the spiritual life? How do we practice it? Psychologically, we need to develop a healthy ego before we can surrender the ego. We have to develop a stable sense of self before we can yield the self.[58] But, to progress on the spiritual journey, we eventually need to relax the grip of self on our lives. We must stop reflexively identifying with the ego. In one of his most powerful essays Merton notes, "Learning to be oneself means, therefore, learning to die in order to live."[59] This sounds dramatic, but it is necessary because when the false self or ego is the primary driver of our personality, we are simply full of ourselves. Our cup of self is full; there is no room for God to enter. Merton writes:

---

[57] Eckhart, *The Complete Mystical Works*, 290.

[58] John McDarch, "The Life of the Self in Christian Spirituality and Contemporary Psychoanalysis," *Horizons* 11, no. 2 (1984): 344–60.

[59] Merton, "Learning to Live," in Cunningham, *Thomas Merton: Spiritual Master,* 359. See also Merton, *New Seeds of Contemplation*, 47; and Thomas Merton, *Wisdom of the Desert* (New York: New Directions, 1960), 7.

The things we really need come to us only as gifts, and in order to receive them as gifts we have to be open. In order to be open we have to renounce ourselves, in a sense we have to *die* to our image of ourselves, our autonomy, our fixation with our self-willed identity. We have to be able to relax the psychic and spiritual cramp which knots us in the painful, vulnerable, helpless "I" that is all we know as ourselves.[60]

ᵢ Merton didn't invent this idea. There are many examples in scripture of the basic Christian truth that we have to die before we live: "For those who want to save their life will lose it, and those who lose their life for my sake will find it" (Mt 16:25); "Therefore we have been buried with him by baptism into death, so that, just as Christ was raised from the dead by the glory of the Father, so we too might walk in newness of life" (Rom 6:4); "Very truly, I tell you, unless a grain of wheat falls into the earth and dies, it remains just a single grain; but if it dies, it bears much fruit" (Jn 12:24); "Blessed are the poor in spirit" (Mt 5:3); "He must increase, but I must decrease" (Jn 3:30); and "Immediately they left their nets and followed him" (Mt 4:20).

Saint Paul, too, declares, "I die every day!" (1 Cor 15:31). While Paul offers a fine example, Jesus's life provides the primary pattern for our spiritual lives. The

---

[60] Merton, *Conjectures of a Guilty Bystander*, 224.

humility he displayed offers a roadmap as we seek to free ourselves from the mental habits that compose the false self. Paul's Letter to the Philippians provides a succinct summary of the path Jesus traveled (2:1–9). The Greek word in Philippians 2:7, translated as "emptied" in the NRSV, is *kenosis*. Cynthia Bourgeault states that kenosis is the key movement of the Christian spiritual life. Instead of clinging to what we have, kenosis is the act of giving it all away, or, as Jesus says, "Do not store up for yourselves treasures on earth" (Mt 6:19). The goal of the kenotic process is to release the grip of the ego on our identity. In a discussion of the theology of Centering Prayer, Bourgeault shares the following quotation from the director of the World Community for Christian Meditation, Laurence Freeman: "Every time we meditate, we participate in the death of Christ."[61] This quotation is the springboard to explain how kenosis is operative in contemplative prayer:

> The practice of meditation is indeed an authentic experience of dying to self—not at the level of the will, however, but at the level of something even more fundamental: our core sense of identity and the egoic processing methods that keep it in place. When we enter meditation, it is like a "mini-death," at least from the perspective of the ego (which is why it can initially feel so scary). We let go of our

---

[61] Cynthia Bourgeault, *Centering Prayer and Inner Awakening* (Boston: Cowley Publications, 2004), 81.

self-talk, our interior dialogue, our fears, wants, needs, preferences, daydreams, and fantasies. These all become just "thoughts," and we learn to let them go. We simply entrust ourselves to a deeper aliveness, gently pulling the plug on that tendency of the mind to want to check in with itself all the time. In this sense, meditation is a mini-rehearsal for the hour of our own death, in which the same thing will happen. There comes a moment when the ego is no longer able to hold us together, and our identity is cast to the mercy of Being itself. This is the existential experience of "losing one's life."[62]

Beyond meditation, we don't have to seek out kenosis. Life brings opportunities to practice it every day. Ruth Burrows writes, "Every day offers small occasions for surrendering self-interest, our own convenience and wishes for the sake of others; for accepting without fuss the disappointments, annoyances, setbacks, humiliations that frequently come our way. The battle is largely fought out in relations with other people."[63] The battle Burrows is talking about here is with the ego. Richard Rohr's definition of suffering, "whenever you are not in control," illustrates this well. We continually suffer because life often eludes our control despite our best efforts. Accepting, rather than

---

[62] Bourgeault, *Centering Prayer and Inner Awakening*, 81.

[63] Ruth Burrows, "Lose Yourself: Getting Past 'Me' to 'Thee,'" *America* 209 (December 2013): 19.

resisting, the roadblocks and frustrations of everyday life is one of the best ways to diminish the grip of the ego. For example, in the Sermon on the Mount, Jesus told his audience not to retaliate against those who threatened them but instead to turn the other cheek. Acceptance is much easier to write about than to put into practice, however, because every time someone pulls out in front of us on the highway or cuts us off on the sidewalk, our anger rises. This anger is the ego asserting its fundamental importance. Why didn't they see *me*? Richard Rohr often says that the false self dies through great love or great suffering, but even small sufferings are opportunities to practice acceptance. The more we can resist the knee-jerk reaction of the ego to the small slights we experience in our everyday interactions with others, the less energy we invest in the external self, and the grip of the false self on us gradually weakens.

WHO AM I?

In conclusion, let us consider how Merton's concept of the true and false self might be useful in our everyday lives. How can it help us comprehend who we really are and how to live in relation to God? The critiques I addressed at the beginning of the chapter testify that, in reality, there is no external or internal self. These terms are just metaphors authors have utilized to help us understand different aspects of our identity. Despite being just metaphors, the concept of the false self is valuable because it helps us recognize the many ways we identify with our superficial self. It helps us see the extent to which we invest our energy in the externals of life (what we will eat, what we will wear, how we compare to those around us). When we understand this process, we see that the external self is not ultimately who we really are. It is not our deepest identity. And when we understand this, an opening is created through which we can become aware of our innate connection to God.

Who am I? For the mystics, the true self is a mirror that, when purified, reflects the divine light.

5

The Experience of God in Scripture and Mystics

In the previous chapter we addressed the scriptural affirmation that God is present in the heart. Despite God being closer to us than we are to ourselves, we are normally unaware of God's presence because we live everyday life on the level of the superficial self or ego. Through the practice of contemplation we can learn how to reduce the mental noise that prevents us from being aware of God's presence. Before we discuss this practice, however, we explore in this chapter how scripture and the mystics describe the experience of the presence of God.

First, the contemplative tradition insists that religious experience is a grace and not an achievement. It is not something we earn through our own efforts. A number of scripture passages affirm the gift of the consciousness of God's presence. Saint Paul provides an obvious example: "For by grace you have been saved through faith, and this is not your own doing; it is the gift of God" (Eph 2:8).

Thomas Keating (1923–2018) points out that this gift is not something that we wait for or search for. It has already been given to every human being. The gift of contemplation is something we awaken to or become conscious of, not something we hope to receive in the future as a reward for the effort we put into contemplative practice.[1]

Scripture depicts the experience of the presence of God in a variety of ways. Some key verses that address the soul's experience of God include the following: "I have been crucified with Christ; and it is no longer I who live, but it is Christ who lives in me" (Gal 2:19–20);[2] "God's love has been poured into our hearts through the Holy Spirit that has been given to us" (Rom 5:5); and "Anyone united to the Lord becomes one spirit with him" (1 Cor 6:17). Some of the most radically unitive language depicting the relationship between God and the soul is found in the Gospel of John. Here, Jesus describes a mutual indwelling, or interpenetration, of himself and the human person: "On that day you will know that I am in my Father, and you in me, and I in you" (Jn 14:20); "The glory that you have given me I have given them, so that they may be one, as we are one, I in them and you in me" (Jn 17:22–23); "I am the vine, you are the branches. Those who abide in me and I in them bear much fruit, because apart from me you

---

[1] Tami Simon, interview with Father Thomas Keating, "Father Thomas Keating: Inviting the Presence of the Divine," *Sounds True: Insights at the Edge*, transcript (2018).

[2] This passage beautifully conveys the relationship between the ego and true self we addressed in Chapter 4.

can do nothing" (Jn 15:5). Other examples from scripture include these: "Then we will see face to face" (1 Cor 13:12); "So that you may be filled with all the fullness of God" (Eph 3:19); and "When he is revealed, we will be like him, for we will see him as he is" (1 Jn 3:2).

Such passages have shaped how the great mystics have described their experiences of the divine.[3] One thing that makes their writing so compelling is the way they use language to articulate their experiences of God. Their descriptions flesh out what it means to become "one spirit" with God. They provide metaphors and images that help us glimpse the intimate relationship between God and the soul. There are many possible examples. Evagrius of Pontus, for example, states: "When minds flow back into him like torrents in the sea, he changes them all completely into his own nature, color, and taste. . . . And as in the fusion of rivers with the sea, no addition in its nature or variation in its color or taste is to be found, so also in the fusion of minds with the Father no duality of natures or quaternity of persons comes about."[4] Bernard McGinn notes that Maximus the Confessor (590–662) "was the first to use three comparisons for union with God repeated

---

[3] Though the language of union, noted above, has been one of the most influential motifs, there have been others as well, such as ecstasy, deification, and endless desire. Bernard McGinn, "Introduction," in *The Essential Writings of Christian Mysticism* (New York: Modern Library, 2006), xv.

[4] M. Parmentier, "Evagrius of Pontus' 'Letter to Melania'" I, *Bijdragen* 46, no. 1 (1985): 13.

by many authors—a drop of water in wine, molten iron in fire, and air in sunshine."[5] In Chapters 2 and 3 we saw that bridal mystics used the imagery of bride and bridegroom in the Song of Songs to describe the relationship between God and the soul. In this tradition Teresa of Avila (1515–82) contrasts a stage of spiritual betrothal in which separation between God and the soul is still possible and spiritual marriage in which "the soul always remains in its center with its God."[6] She writes that spiritual betrothal

> may be symbolized by two wax candles, the tips of which touch each other so closely that there is but one light; or again, the wick, the wax, and the light become one, but the one candle can again be separated from the other and the two candles remain distinct; or the wick may be withdrawn from the wax. But spiritual marriage is like rain falling from heaven into a river or stream, becoming one and the same liquid, so that the river and rain water cannot be divided; or it resembles a streamlet flowing into the ocean, which afterward cannot be disunited from it. This marriage may also be likened to a room into which a bright light enters through two windows—though divided when it enters, the light becomes one and the same.[7]

---

[5] McGinn, *Essential Writings of Christian Mysticism*, 428.

[6] Teresa of Avila, "The Interior Castle 7.1–2," in McGinn, *Essential Writings of Christian Mysticism*, 456.

[7] Teresa of Avila, "The Interior Castle 7.1–2," in McGinn, *Essential Writings of Christian Mysticism*, 456–57.

Angelus Silesius writes: "Who is it can tell the spark within the fire? And who, once within God, can perceive what I am?"[8] Finally, Martin Laird compares our fundamental union with God to the meeting of the Hudson River and the Atlantic Ocean. At the mouth of the river there is no neat dividing line between fresh water and salt water. "The Hudson flows a hundred miles into the Atlantic, while the Atlantic reaches into the freshwater of the Hudson up as far as Newburgh, New York."[9]

How does the experience of the presence of God feel? One of the earliest descriptions of mystical experience in the Christian tradition comes from Bernard of Clairvaux. In Sermon 74 on the Song of Songs he writes:

> And so when the Bridegroom, the Word, came to me, he never made known his coming by any signs, not by sight, not by sound, not by touch. It was not by any movement of his that I recognized his coming; it was not by any of my senses that I perceived he had penetrated to the depths of my being. Only by the warmth of my heart, as I have told you, did I perceive his presence; and I knew the power of his might because .my faults were put to flight and my human yearnings brought into subjection. . . . But

---

[8] Maria Shrady, trans., *Angelus Silesius: The Cherubinic Wanderer* (Mahwah, NJ: Paulist Press, 1986), 95.

[9] Martin Laird, *A Sunlit Absence: Silence, Awareness, and Contemplation* (New York: Oxford University Press, 2011), 64–65.

when the Word has left me, all these spiritual powers become weak and faint and begin to grow cold,
as though you had removed the fire from under a
boiling pot, and this is the sign of his going. Then
my soul is sorrowful until he returns, and my heart
again kindles within me —the sign of his returning.[10]

Bernard illustrates five fundamental characteristics of the
experience of the presence of God. First, it is not sensory;
the experience of God he received was not mediated
through any of his five senses. Second, his experience was
immediate; he received it directly in his heart, his deepest
center. Third, when he experienced God's presence, Bernard mentions that his "human yearnings" were "brought
into subjection." We are reminded, here, of Psalm 131:

> But I have calmed and quieted my soul,
>   like a weaned child with its mother;
>   my soul is like the weaned child that
>   is with me. (v. 2)

Christian mystics have interpreted this verse as a description of the effect mystical experience has on a person.[11] It

---

[10] Louis Dupre and James Wiseman, eds., "Bernard of Clairvaux
(1090–1153)," in *Light from Light: An Anthology of Christian Mysticism*,
2nd ed. (Mahwah, NJ: Paulist Press, 2001), 111.

[11] Evagrius of Pontus, "Admonition on Prayer," in *The Syriac Fathers
on Prayer and the Spiritual Life*, trans. Sebastian Brock (Kalamazoo, MI:
Cistercian Publications, 1987), 71.

conveys that consciousness of the presence of God temporarily stills the grasping activity of the ego. As opposed to the normal restlessness the false self feels, following such an experience we are content with what we have in the moment. Fourth, the experience is transient; it only lasts for a short period of time. Finally, the desire of the soul for God is insatiable. Though in the immediate aftermath of the experience the soul is content, because it has enjoyed such delight in the presence of the bridegroom, the soul soon begins to desire his return.

After we experience God, how then do we understand how we relate to the Divine? Thomas Merton describes the difference between how the mystic comprehends God before and after the experience of presence:

> The reality of God is known to us in contemplation in an entirely new way. When we apprehend God through the medium of concepts, we see Him as an object separate from ourselves, as a being from whom we are alienated, even though we believe that He loves us and that we love Him. In contemplation this division disappears, for contemplation goes beyond concepts and apprehends God not as a separate object but as the Reality within our own reality, the Being within our being, the life of our life . . . the experience of contemplation is the experience of God's life and presence within ourselves not as object but as the transcendent source of our own subjectivity. Contemplation is a mystery in which

God reveals Himself to us as the very center of our own most intimate self. . . . When the realization of His presence bursts upon us, our own self disappears in Him and we pass mystically through the Red Sea of separation to lose ourselves (and thus find our true selves) in Him.[12]

Meditation facilitates a different understanding of the relationship between God and the self. Through the practice of contemplation, mystics cease to interact with God as a separate object and experience God as co-present with their deepest selves (or as their deepest selves). When Merton says God is the "Being within our being" and that we "find our true selves" *in* God, what he means is that instead of becoming aware of an object separate from us to whom we pray, our experience of God in meditation becomes, as Cynthia Bourgeault describes it, an "objectless awareness."[13] According to Martin Laird, "The practice of contemplation amounts to becoming so silent before God that the 'before' drops away. When the 'before' drops away, so do we drop away. We cease to be an object of our own awareness."[14]

---

[12] Thomas Merton, *The New Man* (New York: Farrar, Straus, and Cudahy, 1961), 18–19.

[13] We explore this and the practice of contemplation in more detail in the next chapter.

[14] Martin Laird, *An Ocean of Light: Contemplation, Transformation, and Liberation* (New York: Oxford University Press, 2019), 159.

In other words, rather than relating to God as an external object, through contemplation we become aware of God as a vast open field of selfless connection. Normally, we move through the world attaching positive and negative tags to everything we see and experience. These tags label things as either agreeable or disagreeable to us and narrow our field of vision to the self. In contrast, mystics don't label, judge, or exclude things or other people. Because they are not focused on their own judgments and preferences, their eyes are open to the world around them. The boundaries between things soften. They feel spacious and discover that when they get their "selves" out of the way like this, the connections between them and everything else become apparent. They experience themselves as part of a greater whole.

For Merton, the mystics enter a new awareness of how we relate to God. We find this new relationship expressed poetically in Acts: "In him we live and move and have our being" (17:28). With their gift for language, the mystics can help us imagine what it means to live *in* God. One metaphor they have used is the immense, boundless ocean.[15] Augustine describes our participation in God using the image of a sponge. Like most objects, a sponge has a distinct edge or boundary, but when it is immersed in the ocean, there is water outside of it and inside of it. Water

---

[15] Bernard McGinn, "Ocean and Desert as Symbols of Mystical Absorption in the Christian Tradition," *Journal of Religion* 74, no. 2 (April 1994): 155–81.

indwells every pore and membrane.[16] Similarly, Catherine of Siena (1347–80) writes, "The soul is in God and God in the soul, just as the fish is in the sea and the sea in the fish."[17] Lawrence Kushner describes God as a big circle and the human person as a little circle. Before we encounter the presence of God, we understand the big circle to be far above and separate from the little circle. Through contemplative practice we can experience that our little circle is not outside the big circle but actually inside it.[18] For the mystics, then, it is not possible to be separate from God. God ceases to be an independent object with whom we interact and becomes the spacious, interconnected whole in which we are immersed.

---

[16] Augustine, *Confessions*, trans. Henry Chadwick (New York: Oxford University Press, 1991), 115.

[17] Catherine of Siena, *Catherine of Siena: The Dialogue* (Mahwah, NJ: Paulist Press, 1980), 27.

[18] Lawrence Kushner, "Kabbalah and Everyday Mysticism," On Being with Krista Tippett, transcript (May 15, 2014).

6

Contemplative Prayer

In the discussion on mystical discourse in Chapter 3 we noted that cataphatic and apophatic modes of language are distinct but complementary verbal strategies mystics use to describe who God is. To recap, cataphatic language uses images of God from scripture, liturgy, and tradition to make the Divine seem more relatable. For example, to say that God is like a father or a rock conjures up something in our experience that we can use to relate to the mystery of God. In contrast, apophatic language emphasizes that God is hidden, cannot be seen, and cannot be fully known. Apophatic language insists that God is more than any image can convey; it holds that images conceal more about God than they reveal. The scriptural foundation for apophatic language is Moses's encounter with God at the top of Mount Sinai. During this theophany the mountain was not bathed in light; it was covered in a dark cloud. Gregory of Nyssa uses the imagery of darkness to indicate that the mystery of God cannot be defined through image or metaphor. Ultimately, God is totally incomprehensible; therefore the knowledge mystics gain traveling this path is different from the positive knowledge they acquire through the use of cataphatic language.

Although the two pathways are complementary, we typically begin the spiritual journey traveling the cataphatic way of image and symbol. We ordinarily must reach the end of images before we can move past them. As Thomas Merton maintains, "One cannot go beyond what one has not yet attained."[1] Though most start their spiritual journeys using words and images to relate to God, some reach a stage in which these tools communicate God to them less effectively. At this point, words tediously pile on top of each other and fill all the empty spaces through which the divine light might shine.

In this chapter we consider how one prays when one reaches the end of words and images; we examine teachings on prayer of Christians who approach God through the apophatic path.

Christian teaching on contemplative prayer (or contemplation) begins with Jesus. Not only did he provide fundamental teachings about prayer, but he also put them into practice. In the Gospel of Matthew (6:5–7) Jesus provides two pieces of advice. First, don't make a public display of prayer. Don't engage in it to impress others. Find a place to go where you can be alone with God.

---

[1] Thomas Merton, *Contemplative Prayer* (New York: Image Books, 1996), 84.

"But whenever you pray, go into your room and shut the door and pray to your Father who is in secret; and your Father who sees in secret will reward you" (Mt 6:6). The Greek word *tameion*, which is translated as "room" in the NRSV and "closet" in the KJV, has an outer and an inner meaning in the Orthodox tradition. The outer room is the specific place one goes to be alone. The inner room or closet is the heart.[2] To pray is to descend deep inside yourself where God dwells. The second piece of advice is not to use many words when you pray. This teaching is well suited to the apophatic way; it is fitting for those for whom words drown out rather than connect them to the Divine. Aphrahat, the early fourth-century Persian sage, summarizes the Orthodox interpretation of Jesus's teaching on prayer:

> Our Lord's words tell us to pray in secret, that is in your heart, and to shut the door. What is this door he says we must shut, if not the mouth? For here is the temple in which Christ dwells, just as the apostle said: "You are the temple of the Lord." And Christ comes to enter into your inner self, into this house, to cleanse it from everything that is unclean, while the door (that is your mouth) is closed shut.[3]

---

[2] Igumen Chariton, ed., *The Art of Prayer: An Orthodox Anthology* (New York: Farrar, Straus, and Giroux, 1966), 45–46.

[3] Aphrahat, "*Demonstration IV*, on Prayer," in *The Syriac Fathers on Prayer and the Spiritual Life*, trans. Sebastian Brock (Kalamazoo: MI: Cistercian Publications, 1987), 14. John McGuckin, trans., "Prayer of

Finally, the Synoptic Gospels inform us that Jesus went out alone to pray: "In the morning, while it was still very dark, he got up and went out to a deserted place, and there he prayed" (Mk 1:35; see also Mt 14:23; Lk 5:16; and Lk 6:12).

There are several methods of contemplative prayer. One of the most influential contemporary techniques is Centering Prayer, which follows the following process:

1. Choose a sacred word as the symbol of your intention to consent to God's presence and action within.
2. Sitting comfortably and with eyes closed, settle briefly and silently introduce the sacred word as the symbol of your consent to God's presence and action within.
3. When engaged with your thoughts, return ever-so-gently to the sacred word.
4. At the end of the prayer period, remain in silence with eyes closed for a couple of minutes.[4]

The traditional method of contemplative prayer in Orthodox Christianity is the Jesus Prayer. For centuries Eastern Christians have repeated a version of the prayer, "Lord

---

the Heart in Patristic and Early Byzantine Tradition," in *Illumined in the Spirit* (Yonkers, NY: St. Vladimir's Seminary Press, 2017), 82.

[4] For more information on Centering Prayer, see, for example, the many works of Father Thomas Keating.

Jesus Christ, Son of God, have mercy on me, a sinner." You can use *Jesus* as your sacred word in Centering Prayer as well, or you can choose another short word or phrase that directs your attention to God.

What makes these practices challenging is the way the mind reacts when you attempt to quiet and focus it. As soon as you take away the stimuli that normally keep it occupied, a steady stream of thoughts parade themselves before your mind seeking attention. The Psalmist notes the same phenomenon:

> Be still before the Lord, and wait pa-
>   tiently for him;
>   do not fret over those who prosper in
>   their way,
>   over those who carry out evil devices.
>
> Refrain from anger, and forsake wrath.
>   Do not fret—it leads only to evil.
>   (Ps 37:7–8)

The advice not to fret in this psalm addresses the ubiquitousness of thoughts that plague the practice of contemplative prayer. Theophan the Recluse (1815–94) compares the thoughts that arise during contemplation to mosquitos that annoyingly buzz around one's head in the summertime.[5] And Evagrius Ponticus writes:

---

[5] Chariton, *Art of Prayer*, 162.

The devil so passionately envies the man who prays
that he employs every device to frustrate that purpose. Thus he does not cease to stir up thoughts of
various affairs by means of the memory. He stirs up
all the passions by means of the flesh. In this way he
hopes to offer some obstacle to that excellent course
pursued in prayer on the journey to God.[6]

THOUGHTS

At this point it is necessary to explore how our minds
work because, if we don't understand this process, we
are held captive to it. We suffer because of it. And we
will miss being present to God and the people around
us if we are constantly caught up reacting to our mental
chatter, or as Martin Laird says, our "inner videos."[7] This
chatter is not just present during meditation. Our minds
are continually occupied by feelings and thoughts—the
automatic evaluations of stimuli we generate in our
interactions with our environment, as well as involuntary recurring thoughts—that preoccupy us throughout
the day. We don't consciously initiate these feelings and
thoughts. They arise spontaneously. It is just how our
minds naturally operate.

---

[6] Evagrius Ponticus, *The Praktikos and Chapters on Prayer*, ed. John Eudes
Bamberger (Collegeville, MN: Cistercian Publications, 1972), 62, no. 46.

[7] Martin Laird, "Our Collection of Videos," in *A Sunlit Absence:
Silence, Awareness, and Contemplation* (New York: Oxford University Press,
2011): 25–42.

There are many different kinds of feelings and thoughts. The possibilities are endless. With *feelings* we attempt to hold onto things that cause the pleasant feelings and push away things that cause the unpleasant feelings that arise as we encounter new people and situations. *Thoughts* can often have an obsessive component. A thought I often encounter, for example, is a preoccupation with the next thing I need to do. Another possibility could be a memory of a situation in which we were wronged by someone or a failure for which we haven't forgiven ourselves. It might be an ongoing frustration with our spouse or the next thing we want to buy. It could be an obsession, an addiction, or, for perfectionists like me, something in our life that isn't yet perfect. Thoughts range from rather trivial musings about a favorite sports team to more problematic obsessions involving our most powerful emotions. Martin Laird refers to the beginning stage of the contemplative path in which we are embroiled with our feelings and thoughts as "reactive mind."[8]

Today, psychology is the discipline we turn to in order to understand our thoughts and feelings. Christians, however, have been considering them for centuries. The desert fathers and mothers, in particular, have some very helpful things to teach us about our thoughts.

For a variety of reasons, beginning in the third century, thousands of men and women headed out into the deserts

---

[8] Martin Laird, "Distant Echoes of Home: Reactive Mind," in *An Ocean of Light: Contemplation, Transformation, and Liberation* (New York: Oxford University Press, 2019), 53–94.

of Egypt, Syria, and Palestine to try to live out Paul's exhortation in 1 Thessalonians to "pray without ceasing" (5:17).[9] In their attempts to learn to pray, the desert monks became intimately acquainted with the distracting thoughts that plague contemplative prayer. The monks didn't write long treatises on the spiritual life that carefully articulated the wisdom they had gained. Instead, a younger monk would ask a more experienced one for a "word" of advice, and the memorable sayings were retold until they eventually were written down. The following three examples illustrate three stages in our relationship with thoughts. Our first saying illustrates the first stage:

> A brother said to a hermit, "I don't find any disturbance in my heart." The hermit said, "You are like a door swinging open. Anyone who likes can go inside, and come out again, and you don't notice what is happening. If you had a door that was shut you wouldn't let wicked thoughts come in, and then you would see them standing outside the door and fighting against you."[10]

This is the relationship with thoughts that most people have. If we don't think we are plagued by thoughts, we

---

[9] Douglas Christie, *The Blue Sapphire of the Mind: Notes for a Contemplative Ecology* (New York: Oxford University Press, 2013), 43–44, 74, 114, 123.

[10] Benedicta Ward, trans., *The Desert Fathers: Sayings of the Early Christian Monks* (London: Penguin Books, 2003), 126, no. 43.

don't understand the problem, because who we are *is* our thoughts. Our mind flits from thought to thought throughout the day.

The next saying illustrates the second stage in our relationship with thoughts:

> A brother came to Poemen and said to him, "Many thoughts come into my mind and put me in danger." He sent him out into the open air, and said, "Open your lungs and do not breathe." He replied, "I can't do that." Then Poemen said to him: "Just as you can't stop air coming into your lungs, so you can't stop thoughts coming into your mind. Your part is to resist them."[11]

At this stage we realize we can't stop our thoughts and that we need to defend ourselves against them. At this point, we now understand the problem. But just because we understand the problem, doesn't mean we will attempt to correct it.

This brings us to our third saying:

> A brother who was obsessed by lust came to a famous hermit and said to him, "Of your charity, pray for me, for I am beset by lust." The hermit prayed for him to the Lord. He came a second time to the hermit and said the same words, and again the

---

[11] Ward, *Desert Fathers*, 101, no. 55.

hermit was careful to beseech the Lord on his behalf, and said, "Lord, show me why the devil is doing this work in that brother; I prayed to you, but he has not yet found peace." The Lord showed him what was happening to that brother. He saw the brother sitting down, and the spirit of lust near him playing with him. An angel was standing near to help him and was frowning at that brother because he did not throw himself upon God, but took pleasure in playing with his thoughts, turning towards them. The hermit realized that the chief trouble was in the brother himself. So he said to him, "You are toying with these thoughts." Then he taught him how to reject thoughts like these. The brother's soul revived under the hermit's teaching and prayer, and he found rest from his temptation.[12]

In this story we see a brother who, instead of resisting his thoughts, plays with them. This saying is powerful because it recognizes that it is not the "having" of thoughts that is the problem but rather the way we welcome and indulge them.

Psychologists call the process of toying with our thoughts *rumination*. When we ruminate, we think about something over and over again without taking any positive steps to address the concern. This mental overheating can result in anxiety or insomnia. Yet even if we don't play

---

[12] Ward, *Desert Fathers*, 38–39, no. 19.

with our thoughts so obsessively that it causes us to mentally "overheat," we still spend most of our days moving from one thought to another.

WATCHFULNESS

Evagrius Ponticus was one of the most psychologically perceptive of the desert monks. In his book *The Praktikos*, Evagrius is attentive to how our minds are plagued by thoughts when we try to focus. For him, it is important to "keep careful watch over one's thoughts."[13] When we detect the specific content of the thoughts, we learn more about ourselves, including what we obsess about and what we really want. With this information we grow in self-knowledge and can begin the process of gaining control over our reactions to those thoughts that plague us. One of his eight kinds of "evil" thoughts is *acedia*, which is the temptation to think that anything would be more exciting than what we are doing right now. *Acedia* presents persons who are trying to focus their attention with a more interesting option.[14] It is not unlike when we fantasize about what we will do on the weekend or in our free time when we should be focused on the here and now.

Another Eastern Christian writer who emphasizes the practice of watchfulness or vigilance is Hesychios of Sinai. In his seventh-century work "On Watchfulness and

---

[13] Evagrius Ponticus, *Praktikos,* 29, no. 50.
[14] Evagrius Ponticus, *Praktikos,* 18–19, no. 12.

Holiness," he addresses how to repel the thoughts that plague contemplative practice. Like Poemen and Evagrius, Hesychios recognizes that the natural state of the mind is to be afflicted by thoughts.[15] When a thought appears, the mind is tempted to play with it, "to chase after it and enter into impassioned intercourse with it."[16] Because of the danger the thought poses to inner stillness, it is important to meet it quickly at the entrance of the mind before it has a chance to enter deeply into it and stir it up.[17] For Hesychios, watchfulness involves paying careful attention to whatever the psyche delivers up to consciousness. It is a practice of constant inner vigilance that, when mastered and coupled with repetition of the Jesus Prayer, leads to a stillness of mind and a receptivity to the gift of contemplative awareness.

A variety of biblical texts address the practice of watchfulness or interior vigilance. A good example is "Keep your heart with all vigilance, for from it flow the springs of life" (Prov 4:23; see also Isa 21:6–9; 1 Pet 5:8; Mt 25:13). Evagrius spiritually interpreted Mark 13:33–35 as:

> Be a gatekeeper of your heart and let no thought in without questioning it. Examine every single thought

---

[15] Hesychios the Priest, "On Watchfulness and Holiness," in *The Philokalia: The Complete Text,* vol. 1 (New York: Farrar, Straus, and Giroux, 1983), 182.

[16] Hesychios the Priest, "On Watchfulness and Holiness," 162.

[17] Hesychios the Priest, "On Watchfulness and Holiness," 163.

one by one and ask it: "Are you one of ours or one of our enemies?" And if he belongs to the house, he will fill you with peace. But if he belongs to the enemy, he will confuse you with anger or excite you with desire. Such are the thoughts of the demons.[18]

When we read the text spiritually (as opposed to literally or historically), scripture passages like these convey the urgent importance of guarding our minds from afflictive thoughts.

In the saying above by Poemen, the desert monk states that we need to resist our thoughts. The question is: How do we do this? Evagrius claims that Jesus's encounter with Satan in Matthew 4:1–11 is the model of how we should relate to our constant stream of thoughts. After his baptism and before he called his disciples, Jesus went into the desert, where he fasted for forty days and nights. As he prepared for his public ministry, Satan arrived with three temptations. After each of the temptations, Jesus simply replied with a line of scripture.[19] Jesus's responses to Satan, therefore, offer us a guide to resisting our thoughts; we

[18] Evagrios Pontikos, *Briefe aus der Wüste*, trans. Gabriel Bunge (Trier, Germany: Paulinus-Verlag, 1986), 224. Anselm Gruen, *Heaven Begins within You: Wisdom from the Desert Fathers*, trans. Peter Heinegg (New York: Crossroad, 1994), 91.

[19] Evagrius of Pontus, *Talking Back: A Monastic Handbook for Combating Demons*, trans. David Brakke (Collegeville, MN: Cistercian Publications, 2009), 49.

resist them by not entering into dialogue with them.[20] If we engage the thought, it keeps us wrapped up in our inner chatter. By not taking the bait, we remove the fuel that keeps our mental commentary going. This is why the Centering Prayer guidelines recommend, "When engaged with your thoughts, return ever so gently to the sacred word."

Watchfulness is the primary ascetic struggle of the mystical life. It is the daily, moment-to-moment practice contemplatives engage in to weaken their attachment to their feelings and thoughts. Simone Weil wrote that the ability to focus one's attention helps "destroy the evil in ourselves."[21] The "evil" she speaks of is our innate tendency to grasp and cling to the thoughts that pass through our consciousness, and then to construct our sense of self out of the contents of those thoughts. If we can resist the urge to play with these thoughts, a new awareness greets us on the other side. As Weil notes, "The capacity to drive a thought away once and for all is the gateway to eternity. The infinite in an instant."[22]

In normal everyday consciousness one thought pops into our head, then another, then another. Our attention

---

[20] Martin Laird, *Into the Silent Land: A Guide to the Christian Practice of Contemplation* (New York: Oxford University Press, 2006), 50.

[21] Simone Weil, "Reflections on the Right Use of School Studies with a View to the Love of God," in *Waiting for God* (San Francisco: Harper and Row, 1951), 111.

[22] Simone Weil, *Gravity and Grace* (Lincoln: University of Nebraska Press, 1952), 172.

moves from thought to thought throughout the day. The inability to stop following our thoughts confines us to the exterior surface of life. Maintaining our attention on this running commentary causes us to live on the level of the external self. It distracts us from the silence in our deepest center, the presence of Christ in the heart.

Instead of the false and the true self, when the Eastern Orthodox tradition speaks of the surface and depths of the human person, it uses the language of head and heart. To appreciate this distinction, we need to address, first, the difference between the head and the mind. For the Orthodox, the head represents the rational or thinking part of the human being.[23] It denotes the faculty of reason. The mind (or *nous*) is the spiritual intellect. In its higher ranges it is our receptive spiritual faculty, the "capacity of an intelligent creature for the transcendent encounter with God, in prayer."[24] The *nous* is the part of the human being in which an awareness of God's presence arises, but it is such a sensitive instrument that it only receives a signal once the noise of the body and the rational faculty has been stilled.[25] Second, in the Bible, the heart is not the source of our feelings. It is the center of the entire person. It is where the image of God resides. To pray in the Orthodox tradition, then, is to "bring the mind down from

---

[23] Chariton, *Art of Prayer*, 68.

[24] John McGuckin, *Standing in God's Holy Fire: The Byzantine Tradition* (Maryknoll, NY: Orbis Books, 2001), 171.

[25] John McGuckin, "The Jesus Prayer," *International Journal of Orthodox Theology* 7, no. 1 (2016): 14, 20.

the head into the heart."[26] This descent entails resisting the temptation to grab onto every thought and feeling that emerges into consciousness. When this is practiced over time through a discipline like the Jesus Prayer, our body and mind become calm and we discover that we are not our thoughts. We are the silence that blossoms once we learn to let our thoughts go. With this discovery we experience interior freedom, and an awareness of God's presence emerges. Olivier Clément describes the process using biblical imagery: "The 'descent' into the heart corresponds to Moses's 'ascent' of Sinai."[27] "The heart-spirit is an interior Sinai on which God reveals himself in translucent darkness."[28]

THE FRUITS OF CONTEMPLATIVE PRACTICE

If we practice Centering Prayer (or any other method of contemplation), what can we expect? How will we be changed? In *The Praktikos* Evagrius addresses ascetic practices that prepare the mind for contemplation. As we have noted above, preparation must be made because thoughts thoroughly distract us in our prayer and reinforce our sense of separation from God. For Evagrius, "it is not in our power to determine whether we are disturbed by

---

[26] Chariton, *Art of Prayer*, 105.

[27] Olivier Clément, *The Roots of Christian Mysticism: Texts from the Patristic Era with Commentary*, 2nd ed. (Hyde Park, NY: New City Press, 1993), 246.

[28] Clément, *Roots of Christian Mysticism*, 205.

these thoughts, but it is up to us to decide if they are to linger within us or not and whether or not they are to stir up our passions."[29] The passions are obsessive patterns present in all of us. If we allow the mind to grasp and cling to a thought tailored to one of these obsessive patterns, it whips up an irresistible commentary or "inner video" that takes us far away from the task at hand. Therefore, the intent is not to respond to a thought with more thought. Instead, the goal is to let the thought go so that the process of thinking does not occupy the mind.

Evagrius describes the fruit of the practice of watchfulness as a state of mind he calls *apatheia*, a Greek term that his disciple John Cassian (360–435) rendered in his *Conferences* as "purity of heart."[30] *Apatheia* means freedom from passion. It is a clear, healthy mental state in which the obsessive craving and grasping activity of the mind relaxes. It is a state of equanimity and interior freedom in which we no longer feel like a victim of our thoughts.[31] One of the desert fathers compared this mental state to the calm surface of water. "In the same way as you cannot see your face in troubled water, the soul, if it is not emptied of

---

[29] Evagrius Ponticus, *Praktikos,* 17, no. 6.

[30] In his work Evagrius emphasizes the purified mind, or *nous,* as the locus of contemplative encounter. As the Orthodox tradition developed, the *nous* (or spiritual intellect) came to be located within the heart. John McGuckin, "Prayer of the Heart in Patristic and Early Byzantine Tradition," 59–102.

[31] Evagrius, 31, no. 56; 33–34, nos. 64–67. William Harmless, "The Sapphire Light of the Mind: The *Skemmata* of Evagrius Ponticus," *Theological Studies* 62 (2001): 523, no. 16.

foreign thoughts, cannot reflect God in contemplation."[32] *Apatheia* facilitates "pure prayer," which for Evagrius is the goal of the contemplative life. This state of prayer is the culmination of a process of ascetic purification of the mind, as well as a mind "naked" of concepts and images of God, in which Evagrius says the mind is illuminated by the divine light.[33]

Instead of the imagery of a pure mind (or a pure heart, in the case of John Cassian), Martin Laird refers to the process of mental purification that occurs as a result of a sustained practice of contemplation as "decluttering."[34] For him, we are not fundamentally separate from God. Just like the sun, the light of God is always shining. We can't see the sun on a cloudy day, however, because the clouds obstruct our view. In a similar fashion, what obscures our awareness of the divine light is the clutter in our heads. Laird uses Jesus's saying in the Sermon on the Mount about having a log in our eye to illustrate this obstruction.[35] He assures us that through the practice of contemplation, over time the mind becomes less dominated by inner clutter. As we

---

[32] Clément, *Roots of Christian Mysticism*, 167–68.

[33] Harmless, "*Skemmata*," 521, no. 2; 521, no. 4; 525, no. 23; 526, no. 27. Depicting the experience of God as light is common in Eastern Christianity. See John McGuckin, "Symeon the New Theologian's *Hymns of Divine Eros*: A Neglected Masterpiece of the Christian Mystical Tradition," *Spiritus* 5, no. 2 (Fall 2005): 188. The transfiguration of Christ before the disciples came to be the primary biblical image used to describe contemplative experience in the Christian East.

[34] Laird, *Ocean of Light*, 19–20.

[35] Laird, *Ocean of Light*, 57 (cf. Mt 7:5; Lk 6:42).

sit, the process of letting go of clutter opens up space for the light of God to shine through. In the end the process of decluttering does not completely eliminate thoughts; it changes our relationship with them. Eventually the tight grip of ego relaxes, which allows us to see past our thoughts more easily.[36]

The process of decluttering that Laird describes allows one to experience the vast spaciousness of God. The Psalmist describes the awesome vastness of God:

> Where can I go from your spirit?
>   Or where can I flee from your presence?
> If I ascend to heaven, you are there;
>   if I make my bed in Sheol, you are there.
> If I take the wings of the morning
>   and settle at the farthest limits of the sea,
> even there your hand shall lead me,
>   and your right hand shall hold me fast.
>   (Ps 139:7–10)

A cluttered mind, on the other hand, is a cramped, constricted mind. As we learn to resist grabbing onto every thought that floats down our stream of consciousness, we are able to get a clearer sense of who we really are. We

---

[36] Laird, *Sunlit Absence*, 125.

come to realize we are not the thoughts and preferences that used to preoccupy us. We are not our thoughts; we are the silence present in our deepest center. The noise of our thoughts highlighted our sense of separation from God and other people. When we have learned through the practice of contemplation not to identify with our thoughts, the boundaries we used to feel between ourselves and everything else soften. We feel vast and boundless, like driving in Colorado through a wide, high desert valley under a clear blue sky. Evagrius uses the image of the unboundedness of the heavens to convey the experience of vastness in contemplation: "When the mind has put off the old self and shall put on the one born of grace (cf. Col 3:9–10), then it will see its own state in the time of prayer resembling sapphire or the color of heaven."[37] One of Meister Eckhart's most powerful metaphors suggests that God and the soul share the same ground.[38] In this context, when we experience that our ground (or center or heart) is vast and boundless, we discover that God's ground is as well, and that these grounds coincide.

In his teaching Laird describes the fruit of the practice of contemplation differently from writers such as Bernard of Clairvaux or Mechthild of Magdeburg. In highly

---

[37] Evagrius "On Thoughts," in Robert E. Sinkewicz, *Evagrius of Pontus: The Greek Ascetic Corpus* (New York: Oxford University Press, 2006), 180, no. 39.

[38] Bernard McGinn, "Eckhart and the Mysticism of the Ground," in *The Mystical Thought of Meister Eckhart: The Man from Whom God Hid Nothing* (New York: Crossroad, 2001), 35–52.

personal language inspired by the Song of Songs, Bernard and Mechthild depict union with God as a brief, passionate encounter between a bridegroom and a bride. Laird, on the other hand, describes the ripening of the practice of contemplation as the development of our awareness of God. This awareness, he writes, is the slow unfolding, not of awareness of an object, but of awareness itself:

> The interior silence that all contemplative practices cultivate finally blossoms as luminous, flowing awareness, not awareness of objects that come and go in the mind like changing weather, but the simple opening up from within of the ground of awareness, before it becomes awareness of this or that object. For many, prayer will simply become (whether or not the prayer word is used) just being; simply sitting in awareness.[39]

Cynthia Bourgeault refers to the type of awareness that Laird describes as "objectless awareness." For her, as one's practice develops, one enjoys brief gaps between the thoughts that continually pop into consciousness. She writes:

> In the nanosecond between the cessation of one thought and the arising of the next, there is a moment of pure consciousness where subject and object

---

[39] Laird, *Sunlit Absence*, 14–15.

poles drop out and you're simply *there*. For a nano-
second, there's no "you" and no God. No experience
and no experiencer. There's simply a direct, undivided, sensate awareness of a single, unified field of
being perceived from a far deeper place of aliveness.[40]

Both Evagrius and Martin Laird deftly describe the fruit
of contemplative prayer. They testify that through practice,
our relationship with our afflictive thoughts changes, and
that over time this allows the mirror of our innermost
self to reflect the divine light that is always shining. When
we reach this point, Laird describes the self as "luminous
vastness gazing into luminous vastness."[41] In Chapter 5, we
saw images of water that describe how mystics understand
themselves to be related to God. The aquatic metaphor of
a whirlpool illustrates the contrast between our normal
preoccupation with thoughts and the mystic's awareness
of God.[42] Here, the mind is like a whirlpool spinning in
a river. The act of spinning represents the fact that human beings are "curved in" on themselves. The mind is
wrapped up in its own thoughts and is unaware of what
is going on outside its own drama. At the same time, the

---

[40] Cynthia Bourgeault, *The Heart of Centering Prayer: Nondual Christianity in Theory and Practice* (Boulder, CO: Shambhala, 2016), 130.

[41] Laird, *Ocean of Light*, 59.

[42] Comparative mysticism scholar Jeffrey Kripal uncovered this im-
age in the work of philosopher Bernardo Kastrup. Jeffrey Kripal, *Secret
Body: Erotic and Esoteric Currents in the History of Religions* (Chicago:
University of Chicago Press, 2017), 418.

whirlpool is made of the same substance—water—as the rest of the river. Despite how riveting our thoughts can be, the goal of contemplative practice is to interrupt the spinning mind so it can realize that it is water. It is part of the river.

James uses a similar metaphor of water and waves. When we are trapped in our thoughts, we feel constantly up and down, frequently crashing onto the beach "like a wave of the sea, driven and tossed by the wind" (Jas 1:6–8). Because we are double minded, we feel separate from God, unable to perceive that though we are a wave, we are also connected to the entire ocean.

Thirteenth-century Flemish mystic Hadewijch uses the term *whirlpool* as a cognate of abyss. Beginning in the thirteenth century, medieval writers frequently employed the language of abyss found in Psalm 42:7 to talk about the relationship between God and the soul of the mystic. By using whirlpool as a metaphor for God, Hadewijch suggests a mysterious depth without bottom. For her, this depth conveys the awe-inspiring yet profoundly loving nature of the God with whom she desires to enter into loving union.[43] The way the whirlpool metaphor is employed above reverses the way mystics like Hadewijch used *abyss.* For the medieval mystics, abyss refers to the vast, secret inner depths of God and the human person. Their goal was to unite the two abysses. As used above,

---

[43] Bernard McGinn, "Lost in the Abyss: The Function of Abyss Language in Medieval Mysticism," *Franciscan Studies* 72 (2014): 439–41.

the whirlpool represents those living on the superficial exterior of life, stuck inside their own head, oblivious to the depths inside them. In this case they must interrupt the whirlpool to realize their connection with the rest of the water in the river.

AUTHENTICITY

How do we judge if an experience of the presence of God is authentic? Cynthia Bourgeault distinguishes between states and stages of prayer.[44] Many enjoy fleeting states or experiences of prayer. Taking the long view, they are individual moments on a long journey. But Bernard McGinn insists that mysticism, properly conceived, includes more than just profound experiences. It involves a process, journey, or way of life.[45] All of the disciplines and training in which the mystic engages in preparation to receive such an experience, as well as the transformed life that is the fruit of the encounter, is properly understood as mystical. With mysticism, we are not merely interested in experiences, no matter how profound. It is not about temporary states; the point of the mystical life is a transformation of consciousness that is a fruit of the entire itinerary mystics follow in their journey to God.

---

[44] Bourgeault, *Heart of Centering Prayer*, 45–48.

[45] Bernard McGinn, "Introduction," in *The Essential Writings of Christian Mysticism* (New York: Modern Library, 2006), xiv.

For McGinn, there are three stages on the mystical journey: preparation, attainment, and effect.[46] Preparation indicates the ascetic practices such as watchfulness that mystics engage in. Attainment signals their enjoyment of the gift of presence. It refers to mystics' awareness that their life participates in the life of God. Attainment may seem like a static concept, but mystics' relationship with God is hardly without movement. Because God is infinite (that is, without boundary) and ultimately incomprehensible, God's essence cannot be known. God transcends everything we can know intellectually about God. Jacob's ladder is endless. Simultaneously, the purified soul's desire for God never ceases. No matter how high on the ladder it climbs, it is never sated. It always thirsts for more. Therefore, our relationship with God is not stationary; it offers the possibility of eternal progress or infinite growth that Gregory of Nyssa calls *epektasis*. In Saint Paul's Letter to the Philippians, the Greek word *epektasis* is translated as "straining forward": "Forgetting what lies behind and straining forward to what lies ahead, I press on toward the goal for the prize of the heavenly call of God in Christ Jesus" (Phil 3:13–14). For Gregory, our relationship with God is without limit. He maintains the possibility of never-ending growth.[47]

---

[46] Bernard McGinn, "Christian Mysticism: An Introduction," in *Comparative Mysticism: An Anthology of Original Sources*, ed. Steven T. Katz (New York: Oxford University Press, 2013), 158.

[47] Gregory of Nyssa, *The Life of Moses* (Mahwah, NJ: Paulist Press, 1978), 113–17.

McGinn's third stage of the mystical journey is the effect mystical consciousness produces on the mystic. It is the quality of life mystics display once transformed by the experience of God's presence. This leads us back to the question posed earlier: How do we judge if an experience of God is authentic? Jesus answers our question:

> You will know them by their fruits. Are grapes gathered from thorns, or figs from thistles? In the same way, every good tree bears good fruit, but the bad tree bears bad fruit. A good tree cannot bear bad fruit, nor can a bad tree bear good fruit. Every tree that does not bear good fruit is cut down and thrown into the fire. Thus you will know them by their fruits. By their fruits you shall know them. (Mt 7:16–20)

Similarly, William James (1842–1910) claims that the truth of something is determined by its effects.[48] In his openness to all kinds of religious experiences, James proposes that they should be judged by their results. Has the mystic's mind and life been transformed by what he or she has experienced? If so, then it is authentic.

---

[48] William James, *The Varieties of Religious Experience* (New York: Simon and Schuster, 1997), 35.

7

The Mystical Life

The secular adaptations of mindfulness and yoga widely practiced today help many contemporary people feel more peaceful. By withdrawing attention from our constant stream of thoughts, the practices of watchfulness and contemplation that were outlined in the previous chapter can also help a person feel more centered. Though the rapid pace of society today makes the nurturing of inner peace desirable, following the mystical path is not about cultivating pleasant experiences. These are fine in themselves, when they occur, but they are not the goal of contemplative practice. They are winsome side effects of the process of letting go of self that we do well not to get attached to. Likewise, the contemplative path is not about achieving or gaining something, like a credential or even the title of mystic. Instead, after many seasons of practice, we realize no external self remains to collect the accolade.

We have also noted in the previous chapter that the experience of mystical consciousness (or the ripening of awareness) is not the final stage of the mystical journey, and that, for Bernard McGinn, there are three stages: preparation, attainment, and effect. In this chapter we explore the effect that contemplative practice has on the life of the mystic; that is, how the experience of the presence of God affects the lives of mystics, both in how they view the world and how they act in it. The first part of the chapter addresses interior dispositions. The second part discusses characteristics of mystical action. Interior dispositions or practices protect us from being lost in our thoughts. They prevent us from living on the level of the false self. They are characteristics of the way one perceives the world when one no longer lives on the level of the superficial self.

INTERIOR DISPOSITIONS

The first interior disposition is *seeing nonjudgmentally*. The false or external self sees the world through preferences or filters. As we move through our days, our minds are continually labeling, categorizing, and ranking things. Just as we unconsciously take thousands of breaths per day, our minds involuntarily generate preferences; our fundamental reaction to something is usually whether we like it or not. The danger in this ceaseless generation of mental judgments is that it traps us in our heads and separates us from other people. In effect, the mental labels we attach to things *create* the boundaries we ordinarily sense between the "me" and the "not-me." These labels are what cause us to think that "they" are fundamentally separate from "me."

Instead of the judgments that normally occupy our minds, the mystics recommend a nonjudgmental or non-discriminating way of perceiving the world. One example comes from the desert monks:

> A certain brother inquired of Abbot Pastor, saying: What shall I do? I lose my nerve when I am sitting alone at prayer in my cell. The elder said to him: Despise no one, condemn no one, rebuke no one, God will give you peace and your meditation will be undisturbed.[1]

Another comes from Isaac of Nineveh (613–700):

> And what thou givest, give it with a bountiful eye, and make thy face glad towards him. And give him above what he asks, that which he does not seek. . . . Do not make any distinction between the rich and the poor nor know who is worthy and who is not worthy. . . . Our Lord shared his table with publicans and harlots without making any distinction between those who were worthy and those who were not. . . . Therefore deem all people worthy of bounty and honour, be they Jews or miscreants or murderers.

---

[1] Thomas Merton, *Wisdom of the Desert* (New York: New Directions, 1960), 40.

Especially if they be thy brothers and comrades who have erred from the truth on account of ignorance.[2]

A variety of scriptural texts illustrate aspects of this impartial way of seeing the world:

"You have heard that it was said, 'You shall love your neighbor and hate your enemy.' But I say to you, Love your enemies and pray for those who persecute you, so that you may be children of your Father in heaven; for he makes his sun rise on the evil and on the good, and sends rain on the righteous and on the unrighteous." (Mt 5:43–45)

There is no longer Jew or Greek, there is no longer slave or free, there is no longer male and female; for all of you are one in Christ Jesus. (Gal 3:28)

The eye is the lamp of the body. So, if your eye is healthy, your whole body will be full of light. (Mt 6:22)

The KJV translates the Greek work *haplous* in this verse as "single" instead of "healthy." The single eye is undivided. It takes in the whole without making distinctions.[3] Instead of filtering out or excluding things or people who do not

---

[2] Isaac of Nineveh, *Mystic Treatises*, trans. A. J. Wensinck (Amsterdam: Royal Academy of Sciences, 1923), 38–39.

[3] Carl McColman, *The Little Book of Christian Mysticism* (Charlottesville, VA: Hampton Roads Publishing, 2018), 128, 281–82.

appeal to our preferences, these texts make the case that we should try to see the world nonjudgmentally, as God sees it. If God loves everyone (and even "sends rain on the righteous and on the unrighteous"), so should we.

Cynthia Bourgeault interprets Jesus's parable of the laborers in the vineyard along similar lines.[4] In this parable from Matthew 20 a landowner hires workers at different times of the day to work in his vineyard. At the end of the day, those hired last were paid first. When those who had worked the entire day received the same wage as those who had only worked an hour, they became frustrated. They thought it was unfair that they didn't receive a bonus because they had worked many more hours under the hot sun. This parable is challenging because when we read it, we tend to agree with the grumbling workers. To the mind that is constantly judging and discriminating, it *is* unfair that those who worked harder were not compensated more for their effort. This parable suggests that God plays by a different set of rules than us. In human society there is no free lunch. In contrast, the landowner, who represents God, exhibits a nonjudging mind. He says, "I choose to give to this last the same as I give to you. Am I not allowed to do what I choose with what belongs to me? Or are you envious because I am generous?" (Mt 20:14–15). God loves everyone. God wants everyone to have enough, regardless of how responsible or hardworking they are.

---

[4] Cynthia Bourgeault, *Wisdom Jesus* (Boulder, CO: Shambhala, 2008), 38–39.

This is difficult for those of us who are responsible and hardworking because these, in fact, are important values. As admirable as these values are, however, this parable suggests they prevent us from seeing how God sees. They fixate us on how people differ and prevent us from seeing how they are connected.

The second interior disposition is *acceptance*, which is related to the first. When we judge the world around us, we assert that it fails to conform to our standard of what we want it to be. We reject it as it is. To accept the world is to move through it without immediately labeling, judging, or categorizing it. It is to encounter it directly without the filter of the discriminating mind. Paul tells the Thessalonians: "Give thanks in all circumstances" (1 Thess 5:18). This is easier to say than to do, but both Jesus and Paul embraced this fundamental openness to the present moment.

In the garden of Gethsemane, when the violent consequences of the path he was taking were about to engulf him, Jesus prayed, "Father, if you are willing, remove this cup from me; yet, not my will but yours be done" (Lk 22:42). After an ecstatic experience Paul records that he was given a "thorn in the flesh" (2 Cor 12:7) to keep him humble. He does not explain what this "thorn" was, but he prayed three times for it to be removed. When God failed to honor his request, Paul describes his acceptance of the situation: "Therefore I am content with weaknesses, insults, hardships, persecutions, and calamities for the sake of Christ; for whenever I am weak, then I am strong" (2 Cor 12:10).

The root of sin for Meister Eckhart is the attachment to our will. The remedy is an attitude of detachment. Detachment for Eckhart is an acceptance of what is—a yes to whatever arises, whether it is agreeable or disagreeable. To be detached is to let go of our preference in the current situation. This is the poverty of spirit about which Eckhart writes in his famous Sermon 52; in an earlier work he gives the following example:

> And that I consider better than anything, that a man should fully abandon himself to God when He would cast anything upon him, be it disgrace, trouble, or whatever kind of suffering it might be, accepting it with joy and gratitude, allowing oneself rather to be led by God than plunging into it oneself. So just learn all things gladly from God and follow him, and all will go well with you. In that way you can well take honor or comfort, but in such a way that, if discomfort and dishonor were to be a man's lot, he would likewise be able and willing to bear them. *Then* they may rightly and legitimately feast, who would have been as ready and willing to fast.[5]

Acceptance is the disposition with which we should encounter each new moment. This does not mean that we should acquiesce to whatever is present in that moment

---

or that we should consent to injustice. Belden Lane writes, "The truest impulse toward work for social justice, there- fore, grows not out of an anxious sense of pity for others or a grandly noble desire to serve, but out of the abandon- ment of the self in God. A love that works for justice is wholly uncalculating and indifferent, able to accomplish much because it seeks nothing for itself."[6] To be human is to act. Acceptance keeps the ego out of the way so we can appropriately respond to the situation at hand. It helps prevent our response from being motivated by self-interest, fear, anger, or revenge.

The third interior disposition is not *categorizing* people into opposing groups. One way that human beings formu- late their identity is by establishing who they are not (or what they oppose). On the one hand, in-groups construct their identity by clearly identifying those who are differ- ent from them. Through the process of "othering," the in-group determines that the "other" possesses a trait or characteristic that the in-group wishes to exclude from its tribe. This creates a distinct identity for the in-group but results in the stigmatization of those outside. Othering is a mechanism through which in-groups fashion an identity by deciding, often on an arbitrary basis, that specific others do not belong.

Mystics, on the other hand, experience that they are not separate from others but rather one with all. Scripture and

---

[6] Belden Lane, *The Solace of Fierce Landscapes: Exploring Desert and Mountain Spirituality* (New York: Oxford University Press, 1998), 76.

the contemplative tradition provide a variety of metaphors and images that help us see how people are connected rather than fundamentally separate or opposed. One characteristic of Paul's letters is that he addresses them to churches; other than Philemon, his writings are addressed to groups, not individuals. In 1 Corinthians he is concerned about the divisions that had formed between rival factions in the young church he had founded in Corinth. After discussing many of these divisions, he advocates unity in the congregation through his metaphor of the body of Christ. Here, he compares the church to the human body. Some parts of the body are more high profile than others. Not everyone can be an eye or a hand, but everyone has a role to play. Without a foot, knee, or ankle, a person couldn't walk around. All of our parts are indispensable to a fully functioning body. The key verse reads, "If one part of the body suffers, every part suffers with it" (1 Cor 12:26). This verse uses the common experience of physical illness to illustrate that human beings in the church are interconnected. When this text is read spiritually, it reveals that the interconnectedness is not only true in the church, but also among the entire human family, and the natural world as well.

The mystics likewise emphasize the connectedness of the human race. Evagrius Ponticus writes, "A monk is a man who considers himself one with all men because he seems constantly to see himself in every man."[7] Martin

---

[7] Evagrius Ponticus, *The Praktikos and Chapters on Prayer,* ed. John Eudes Bamberger (Kalamazoo, MI: Cistercian Publications, 1972), 76, no. 125.

Laird has recovered the metaphor of the wheel from the early church to explain our relatedness to others. In this image the hub of the wheel represents God. The spokes represent humankind. At the rim of the wheel the spokes are furthest apart. As we move toward to the hub, the spokes come closer together. For Laird, "The more we journey toward the Center, the closer we are both to God and to each other."[8] The closer we move toward our center, the less distant our brothers and sisters seem from us. In the center, we realize we are all connected in the body of Christ.

Thomas Merton's most frequently discussed religious experience also conveys this insight. At the corner of Fourth and Walnut Streets in Louisville, he writes, "in the center of the shopping district," he "was suddenly overwhelmed with the realization that I loved all those people."[9] Before this epiphany he understood the contemplative life he lived in the monastery to be more holy than the life of an ordinary lay person. In his mind he distinguished between the life he was living and the lives of those outside the cloister. He describes this moment of understanding as "like waking from a dream of separateness, of spurious self-isolation in a special world, the world of renunciation and supposed holiness."[10] Be-

---

[8] Martin Laird, *Into the Silent Land: A Guide to the Christian Practice of Contemplation* (New York: Oxford University Press, 2006), 12.

[9] Thomas Merton, *Conjectures of a Guilty Bystander* (New York: Image Books, 1989), 156.

[10] Merton, *Conjectures of a Guilty Bystander*, 156.

fore this moment he had looked down on people in the world; now he felt connected to them. In his new vision of humanity Merton no longer saw his life as separate from those outside the cloister. He had awakened to the fact that he was living in "the same world as everybody else" and now felt "one with them."[11]

For Merton, we develop an awareness of our connectedness to others in solitude. In his essay "Notes for a Philosophy of Solitude" he makes three points about the connection between solitude and one's relationship to other people. First, he asserts that solitude is not a rejection of society. It is, however, a withdrawal from the distractions and collective illusions of the surrounding culture.[12] Merton observes that most people do not enjoy being alone. Therefore society is happy to provide "bread and circuses" that allow them to remain immersed in the crowd and "avoid [their] own company for twenty-four hours a day."[13] Such illusions are beliefs internalized from one's social group, which in his day included "racial hatreds" and the practice of justifying the self and demonizing one's enemy.[14] Second, those who live truly solitary lives live in unity with the self and God. In order to experience unity within the self, they must renounce the collective illu-

---

[11] Merton, *Conjectures of a Guilty Bystander*, 157, 158.

[12] Thomas Merton, "Notes for a Philosophy of Solitude," in *Thomas Merton: Selected Essays*, ed. Patrick F. O'Connell (Maryknoll, NY: Orbis Books, 2013), 76.

[13] Merton, "Notes," 66.

[14] Merton, "Notes," 70, 67.

sions of their social group and become empty of them.[15] Rather than asserting the self, they must die to the false social self and live in harmony with their deepest self, "lost in God and lost to himself."[16] Third, the empty self is not only united with itself and with God; it is also united with other people.[17] Merton explains how in solitude one may be paradoxically united with others by distinguishing a shallow "I" from a deep or inner "I." On the one hand, for the shallow "I," there may exist a "facade of apparent unity" at certain moments, but there is no unity on a deeper level.[18] The inner "I," on the other hand, is shared by everyone.[19] It is universal, "for in this inmost 'I' my own solitude meets the solitude of every other man and the solitude of God."[20] This inner "I" is not only the deepest part of the self, it "is Christ Himself, living within us."[21] Therefore in true solitude, solitary persons find that at the level of the inner "I," they are united with God and with other people.

---

[15] Merton, "Notes," 70.

[16] Merton, "Notes," 82.

[17] For more on this theme in Merton's writings, see John Teahan, "Solitude: A Central Motif in Thomas Merton's Life and Writings," *Journal of the American Academy of Religion* 50 (December 1982): 521–38; and Douglas Burton-Christie, "The Work of Loneliness: Thomas Merton's Experiments in Solitude," *Anglican Theological Review* 88, no. 1 (Winter 2006): 25–45.

[18] Merton, "Notes," 73.

[19] Merton, "Notes," 73.

[20] Merton, "Notes," 85.

[21] Merton, "Notes," 85.

As a black man coming of age in the first half of the twentieth century in the United States, Howard Thurman's (1899–1981) experience of his fellow human beings was often quite different from the ecstatic exuberance Merton displayed in his Fourth and Walnut epiphany. When Thurman was growing up, segregation was the institutional policy of the nation. African Americans were treated as second-class citizens in ways sanctioned by state and federal law. The policies of segregation didn't begin coming down until the Supreme Court's 1954 *Brown vs. Board of Education* decision that declared that "separate educational facilities are inherently unequal." The issue that Thurman spent much of his adult life writing about was how African Americans could utilize spiritual resources to develop their inner lives in order to withstand the corrosive effects of prejudice and discrimination.

One of Thurman's most powerful pieces is his 1963 essay "Reconciliation." The goal of the practice of reconciliation is to restore harmony between two parties. Before reconciliation can be accomplished at the interpersonal level, he claims, individuals must first experience an inner reconciliation. They need to experience interior wholeness before they can establish harmonious relations with others. We do not achieve this inner wholeness on our own, however. We only experience it through the care and concern provided by another person. Thurman's central claim is that "every man wants to be cared for . . . to know that . . . he is not alone, but the object of another's concern and caring."[22] When this does not happen, "when the need to be cared for is dishonored, threatened, or undermined, then the individual cannot experience his own self as a unity and his life may become deeply fragmented and splintered."[23] On a fundamental level, if we don't have someone who accepts and understands us, we have no foundation. We feel divided within, and our mental health suffers.

After he addresses the experience of harmony within the self, Thurman moves to the social realm. In situations when one is targeted by violence, the method of reconciliation he advocates is nonviolence. He defines nonviolence as "a response to a violent act, directed toward oneself in the first place, in a manner that meets the need of the individual to be cared for, rather than the apparent nature of the act itself."[24] As we noted, Thurman firmly believes that every human being has a fundamental need to be cared for. A nonviolent response to a violent act can facilitate reconciliation because it recognizes that the violent act itself is not the primary intent of the perpetrator.[25] For Thurman, "The violent act is the desperate act. It is the demand of a person to force another to honor his desire and need to be cared for, to be understood. In this sense

---

[22] Howard Thurman, "Reconciliation," in *Disciplines of the Spirit* (Richmond, IN: Friends United Press, 1963), 105.

[23] Thurman, "Reconciliation," 107.

[24] Thurman, "Reconciliation," 111–12.

[25] Thurman, "Reconciliation," 111.

the violent act is a plea, a begging to have one's need to belong fulfilled and confirmed."[26]

How does nonviolence work? If one answers violence with violence, the situation of conflict between the two parties remains. Both sides are confirmed in the rightness of their position, and the situation escalates. But if victims of violence are strong enough not to respond, this compels the perpetrators to face their own behavior.[27] It forces them to examine the suffering they are causing others through their violent actions. Nonviolence is a powerful tool of reconciliation because it "creates and maintains a climate in which the need to be cared for and understood can be honored and effectively dealt with."[28] When victims of violence display a nonviolent attitude, they courageously maintain an openness to the desire to be understood that perpetrators are trying to communicate through their acts of violence.[29]

Thurman recommends nonviolence, but he understands that it is hard. It is hard not to respond because it is human nature to defend ourselves.[30] Not only is not retaliating hard, but refusing to resort to hatred of the perpetrator is also hard. When we are being attacked, when we are being willed out of existence, hating our attacker serves

---

[26] Thurman, "Reconciliation," 112.

[27] Thurman, "Reconciliation," 115.

[28] Thurman, "Reconciliation," 114.

[29] Thurman, "Reconciliation," 115.

[30] Thurman, "Reconciliation," 116.

a protective function; it is a way of affirming ourselves. It is a way of preserving our fundamental self-worth when we are under threat, but it also eats away at us from the inside.[31] Ultimately, Thurman advocates not hating the aggressor because hate closes us off from them. It prevents us from trying to understand where they are coming from, what they need, and what they are looking for in the current situation.

It is only at this point that Thurman addresses religious experience:

> In religious experience, a man has a sense of being touched at his inmost center, at his very core, and this awareness sets in motion the process that makes for his integration, his wholeness. . . . The experience of God reconciles all the warring parts that are ultimately involved in the life of every person as against whatever keeps alive the conflict, and its work is healing and ever redemptive.[32]

Experiencing the presence of God makes us feel completely cared for. The love we receive resolves our internal conflicts, which allows us to experience harmony within ourselves. At the same time, Thurman insists, this religious experience is not for ourselves alone. It also carries an ethical imperative that we must give to others what we have

---

[31] Thurman, "Reconciliation," 113.
[32] Thurman, "Reconciliation," 121.

received from God. Because we have felt understood and cared for by God, we must offer the same to our fellows.[33]

Consequently, Thurman's proposal to end segregation isn't grand or dramatic. He simply wants people to try to understand one another. He wants ordinary people, black and white, to spend time together and get to know each other in a relaxed, unhurried way. Only then can we learn how to care for this person who initially seems so different from us, because we discover that the other person has the same need to be cared for and appreciated that we do.[34]

A concrete practice to help bring down barriers between people is the simple act of listening. The desert fathers and mothers were very sensitive to the trouble our tongues can get us into.

> A brother said to Abba Poemen, "If I see something, do you want me to tell you about it?" The old man said to him: "It is written: 'If one gives answer before he hears, it is his folly and shame' (Prov 18:13). If you are questioned, speak; if not, remain silent."[35]

In contrast, many people today love nothing more than telling others what they think. The giving of opinions is so popular that large numbers even enjoy it as entertainment. Millions of people watch pundits give "hot takes" on

---

[33] Thurman, "Reconciliation," 122.

[34] Thurman, "Reconciliation," 127.

[35] Benedicta Ward, *The Desert Christian: Sayings of the Desert Fathers: The Alphabetical Collection* (New York: Macmillan, 1975), 173, 45.

cable news and listen to radio hosts pontificate. Many of these news outlets, however, are echo chambers in which specific groups of people rehearse to one another what the rest of the world is like without actually exploring the experience of those outside their tribe. Opinions get repeated within these cultural groups so often that the people in these communities believe them, regardless of whether or not they correspond to reality.

An antidote to these echo chambers is the simple act of listening to the experience of people outside our group. To love our neighbor we need, at least, to listen to their experience. If the only people we ever talk to or listen to share our worldview, it is impossible to understand those from other communities because everyone's experience differs. In other words, we need to have conversations with people who are different from us, or at least engage in reading that explores the experience of other communities. Love of neighbor requires that we listen to the experience of others before we give our opinion about *their* experience.

The best learning experience I've had around issues of race has been sharing an office at my current institution with a Latinx philosopher. Listening to my friend share his experience of being a person of color has opened my eyes to the reality of race and white privilege. When I first heard the term *white privilege,* I was confused because I certainly did not feel privileged. I grew up in a small town in West Virginia. My grandfather was a coal miner. I completed my undergraduate degree at a public university.

Listening to Edgar, I now appreciate that privilege isn't solely about income level. As my education continues, I realize that I am fundamentally privileged simply because strangers aren't immediately suspicious of me because of the color of my skin.

Listening can help us understand another person's experience, and it can also help speakers understand themselves more deeply. Douglas Steere's "On Listening to Another" explores the dynamics involved in "listening and being listened to."[36] He thinks it is possible, through the quality of one's listening, to help others understand themselves better and even cultivate an awareness of God. When we need to share something with a trusted friend, we can tell when that friend isn't truly listening to us. We intuitively perceive this because of the presence of what Steere calls the "inward spectator listener" *within each speaker.*[37] The spectator-listener is the unconscious part of us that notices if our friend really cares about what we are saying. If instead of listening our friend is just waiting to talk, the conversation steers toward surface matters. If our friend does care, the inward spectator-listener recognizes that it is safe to open up. Listening deeply involves projecting interest in what the speaker is saying, caring for his or her well-being, and accepting rather than judging. This creates

[36] Douglas Steere, "On Listening to Another," in *Doubleday Devotional Classics,* vol. 3, ed. E. Glenn Hinson (New York: Doubleday, 1978), 204.

[37] Steere, "On Listening to Another," 209, 211.

a healthy climate for self-disclosure in which the speaker is encouraged to express the concern that lies deep inside. Due to the quality of the listening, an attentive listener is even able to bring out more from the speaker than the speaker consciously knew was there. For Steere, such a climate is rare, but when a listener creates it, it is "almost the greatest service that any human being ever performs for another."[38]

CHARACTERISTICS OF MYSTICAL ACTIVITY

Because mysticism is not a form of passivity or withdrawal from the tasks of everyday life, we conclude with four characteristics of how mystics act in the world. With their minds clear of mental clutter, we ask, how do mystics relate to other people and the world around them?

The first characteristic of the contemplative life is that salvation—heaven or life with God—is not a future state; it happens in the *present moment*. It is common for people to use God as an insurance policy against misfortune, either in this life or the next. From this perspective God is relevant insofar as God is useful. Bernard of Clairvaux illustrates this approach with the second of his four stages of the mystical journey: love of God *for self's sake*.[39] One problem with this understanding is that our interactions

---

[38] Steere, "On Listening to Another," 214.

[39] Gillian Evans, *Bernard of Clairvaux: Selected Works* (Mahwah, NJ: Paulist Press, 1987), 193.

with God only occur on occasions when we really need God—for example, when we lose our job, our relationship falls apart, or we get diagnosed with a serious disease. If God's services are not currently required, we put God on a shelf to be pulled down later when needed. The good news in such circumstances is that God is always available. God is present in the ordinary, everyday moments of our lives if we simply turn and open ourselves to God. For example, as Matthew states, "From that time Jesus began to proclaim, 'Repent, for the kingdom of heaven has come near'" (Mt 4:17). In this verse heaven is not a future state; God reigns in the present moment. Brian Pierce makes a similar point in relation to Moses's encounter with God in the burning bush in Exodus 3:1–15. In this theophany God says to Moses "I Am," which indicates that God is present in the "here and now."[40]

The Gospel of Luke states: "Once Jesus was asked by the Pharisees when the kingdom of God was coming, and he answered, 'The kingdom of God is not coming with things that can be observed; nor will they say, "Look, here it is!" or "There it is!" For, in fact, the kingdom of God is among you'" (Lk 17:20–21)[41] Jim Marion claims that the kingdom of heaven Jesus preached is not a place where Christians reside after death. Based on a common

---

[40] Brian Pierce, *We Walk the Path Together* (Maryknoll, NY: Orbis Books, 2005), 28.

[41] Note also the Gospel of Thomas: "The kingdom of the father is spread over the earth, and people do not see it" (Saying 113).

translation of Luke 17:21, he claims the kingdom must be realized "within" ourselves. The kingdom of heaven is a level of human consciousness that recognizes no separation between God and human beings (or between fellow human beings), and for Marion this level of awareness must be cultivated during our lifetimes.[42] In each of these sources heaven is not solely a future reality; the point of religious life is to experience it in the present moment. The goal is to participate in the building up of the kingdom of God on earth now instead of thinking that our religious life will only be fulfilled in the future, after our death.

A second characteristic of the contemplative life is that it is important, but it *does not have priority over the active life*. For those familiar with the Christian tradition, this seems like common sense. A powerful illustratation of this point is found in 1 John: "Those who say, 'I love God,' and hate their brothers or sisters, are liars; for those who do not love a brother or sister whom they have seen, cannot love God whom they have not seen. The commandment we have from him is this: those who love God must love their brothers and sisters also" (1 Jn 4:20–21). The desert fathers and mothers also emphasized this:

> A brother said to one of the elders, "Here are two brothers. One never leaves his cell where he prays,

---

[42] Jim Marion, *Putting on the Mind of Christ: The Inner Work of Christian Spirituality* (Charlottesville, VA: Hampton Roads Publishing, 2011), 33, 39–40.

fasts for six days at a time, and gives himself up to all sorts of mortification. The other looks after the sick. Which of the two lives a life more pleasing to God?"

The elder replied, "The brother who fasts for six days on end would not be the equal of the one who looks after the sick, not even if he hanged himself by the nose."[43]

Despite the clear guidance of these sources, some in the contemplative tradition have felt a tension between the demands of the love of God and love of neighbor. This tension is illustrated by the way these writers interpret the story of Mary and Martha in Luke 10:38–42. In this story the two sisters are entertaining Jesus in their home. While Martha attends to the needs of their guests, Mary sits at the feet of Jesus listening to his teaching. When Martha asks Jesus to tell Mary to help her, Jesus replies to Martha, "Mary has chosen the better part, which will not be taken away from her." For monastic writers such as John Cassian, Gregory the Great, Bernard of Clairvaux, and the author of *The Cloud of Unknowing,* this passage from scripture indicates that the contemplative life is of higher importance to the monk than the active life. As the tradition developed—especially with the rise of the mendicant orders, the Franciscans and Dominicans—others came to

---

[43] Olivier Clément, *The Roots of Christian Mysticism: Texts from the Patristic Era with Commentary*, 2nd ed. (Hyde Park, NY: New City Press, 1993), 280.

different views about the best way to live out one's calling from God. One of those who upheld the importance of the active life was the Dominican friar Meister Eckhart. He creatively reads this story and reverses the traditional monastic interpretation. Instead of praising Mary and the contemplative life, Eckhart praises Martha for her maturity and effectiveness in uniting contemplation and action through the performance of good works. He interprets Martha's complaint to Jesus as her desire for Mary to move past the sweetness she experiences in the words of Jesus so she might grow in her faith by putting love into action.[44]

Thomas Merton argues that the goal of the spiritual life should be a balance between contemplation and action.[45] He criticizes as "quietism" interpretations of contemplation that isolate one from one's fellow human beings:

> One of the worst illusions in the life of contemplation would be to try to find God by barricading yourself inside your own soul, shutting out all external reality by sheer concentration and will-power, cutting yourself off from the world and other men by stuffing yourself inside your own mind and closing the door like a turtle.

---

[44] Meister Eckhart, "Selections from Sermon 86," in *The Essential Writings of Christian Mysticism*, ed. Bernard McGinn (New York: Modern Library, 2006), 529.

[45] Thomas Merton, *Contemplative Prayer* (New York: Image Books, 1996), 66.

Fortunately most of the men who try this sort of thing never succeed. For self-hypnotism is the exact opposite of contemplation. We enter into possession of God when He invades all our faculties with His light and His infinite fire. We do not "possess" Him until He takes full possession of us. But this business of doping your mind and isolating yourself from every thing that lives, merely deadens you. How can fire take possession of what is frozen?[46]

For Merton, contemplation along these lines is an illusion. It is fundamentally a narcissistic exercise. "He is not alone with God, but alone with himself."[47] "It is purely the nothingness of a finite being left to himself and absorbed in his own triviality."[48]

A third characteristic of the contemplative life is that not only does it enable action, it enables *selfless action*. One way that contemplation fosters selfless action is by helping us see the world more clearly. Martin Laird claims that the opposite of the contemplative life is not the active life but rather the reactive life.[49] To the extent that our consciousness is embroiled in reacting to the constant stream of

---

[46] Thomas Merton, *New Seeds of Contemplation* (New York: New Directions, 1961), 64.

[47] Merton, *Contemplative Prayer*, 90.

[48] Merton, *Contemplative Prayer*, 90.

[49] Martin Laird, *A Sunlit Absence: Silence, Awareness, and Contemplation* (New York: Oxford University Press, 2011), 42.

thoughts in our heads, the only thing we have to offer the
world is our mental clutter. And when we are preoccupied
with our own thoughts, we have difficulty recognizing the
needs of our neighbor. In her classic essay on school studies and attention, Simone Weil writes about how we can
only help those around us if we actually see them:

> The soul empties itself of all its own contents in
> order to receive into itself the being it is looking at,
> just as he is, in all his truth. Only he who is capable
> of attention can do this. So it comes about that, para-
> doxical as it may seem, a Latin prose or a geometry
> problem, even though they are done wrong, may
> be of great service one day, provided we devote the
> right kind of effort to them. Should the occasion
> arise, they can one day make us better able to give
> someone in affliction exactly the help required to
> save him, at the supreme moment of his need.[50]

To follow Christ, we must put the love we receive
from God into action. This does not mean just any action,
however. This is not the place to discuss discernment in
depth, but the practice of contemplation is a component
of the process of discernment because it uncovers our
motivations for action. It helps us see what we want to

---

[50] Simone Weil, "Reflections on the Right Use of School Studies
with a View to the Love of God," in *Waiting for God* (New York: Harper
and Row, 1951), 115.

do and *why* we want to do it. In contemplative practice, as Robert Kennedy, SJ, notes, we "sit until the self falls off."[51] As we sit, aspects of ourselves emerge into consciousness as thoughts. When these thoughts coalesce as concerns, desires, fears, regrets, nostalgias, and plans, teachers of contemplation counsel us not to engage them. After our sit is over, however, we would do well to sift through the thoughts and ask: What do they reveal about myself? What are they disclosing about what is really important to me right now? What am I trying to get *for myself* out of the current project I am working on? Thomas Merton adds the following advice about how meditation can contribute to the process of discernment:

> What is the relation of this [contemplation] to action? Simply this. He who attempts to act and do things for others or for the world without deepening his own self-understanding, freedom, integrity, and capacity to love, will not have anything to give others. He will communicate to them nothing but the contagion of his own obsessions, his aggressiveness, his ego-centered ambitions, his delusions about ends and means, his doctrinaire prejudices and ideas. There is nothing more tragic in the modern world than the misuse of power and action.[52]

---

[51] Tracy Cochran, "To Live with Gratitude, an Interview with Robert Kennedy, SJ, Roshi," *Parabola* 33, no. 1 (Spring 2008).

[52] Lawrence Cunningham, ed., *Thomas Merton: Spiritual Master, The Essential Writings* (Mahwah, NJ: Paulist Press, 1992), 375.

A fourth characteristic of the contemplative life is that loving one's neighbor involves *becoming a conduit of God's love.* Augustine claimed that we are curved in on ourselves. This is true in all aspects of our lives, but fundamentally it is true of our thoughts. We are usually so wrapped up in the involuntary thoughts that pop into our heads, one after the other, that this mental clutter inhibits our consciousness of God and of other people. Our inclination to grasp these thoughts continually is the cloud that obstructs our view of the light of God. The goal of the spiritual life is to remove the metal clutter that obscures our awareness of God. The objective is to empty ourselves, to remove that which blocks the flow of God's love energies that are present in, and constantly moving through, everything. When these blockages have been released through seasons of contemplative practice, we experience an inner spaciousness and freedom that allows us to participate consciously in this circulation of love.

Scripture and the mystics provide various images and metaphors to help us envision how God's love moves through everything. In each moment God is the source of the love and compassion that pour into the universe. As Christians, we understand God to be a Trinity of relations. The three Persons circulate love among themselves, and this love boils over and is shared with the rest of the creation. In scripture the heart is not the center of the emotions; it is the center of the entire person. Saint Paul claims that God's love flows into us through the heart: "God's love has been poured into our hearts through the

Holy Spirit that has been given to us" (Rom 5:5). The experience of this love is precious, but God does not intend the flow to stop here. Jesus succinctly explains how God intends the love to proceed: "As the Father has loved me, so I have loved you" (Jn 15:9). Therefore, we receive the love of God in our deepest center in order to pass it on to others. The goal of the process is to become part of the flow.

Mechthild of Magdeburg uses various images to describe the flowing nature of God's love: water, milk, wine, blood, tears, honey, molten gold, and light.[53] These flowing liquids connect God and the soul and represent the gift we share with others. To depict the process of passing on what we have received, she describes the human person as a cup or vessel:

> The great outflow of divine love that never ceases flows on and on unceasingly and effortlessly in such a sweet course unfailingly that our tiny vessel becomes full and brims over. If we do not block it with self-will, our small vessel is always overflowing with God's favor.
>
> Lord, you are full and you fill us as well with your favor. You are great and we are small. How shall we be like you? Lord, you have given us much and we should pass it on in turn. . . . We are, alas, so tiny that

---

[53] Carol Flinders, *Enduring Grace: Living Portraits of Seven Women Mystics* (San Francisco: HarperOne, 1993), 53.

a single little word from God or Holy Scripture fills us so completely that for the moment we can take in no more. Then we pour the gift back again into the large container that is God. How are we to do this? In holy longing we should pour it over sinners that they be cleansed. . . . If it again becomes full, we should pour it over the distress of poor souls who are in torment in purgatory. . . . Our Lord God loved us first of all. He also toiled for us first and foremost. . . . We should give him the same in return if we want to be like him.[54]

In this excerpt Mechthild explains how we participate in God's love for the universe. God ceaselessly pours out love into the creation. If our hearts are open, God's love flows into us. Our goal should not be to revel in enjoyment of our full cup, however. Instead, we should imitate God by pouring out our abundance of love on our neighbors in need. When we do this, our cup does not remain empty but is filled continuously because God's nature is to fill us with love.

Having addressed various ways mystics respond to the experience of the presence of God, we now consider the context for the contemplative life—the environment. How do mystics understand themselves to be related to the natural world?

---

[54] Mechthild of Magdeburg, *The Flowing Light of the Godhead* (Mahwah, NJ: Paulist Press, 1997), 324.

8

Mysticism and the Natural World

In 1967, medieval historian Lynn White published an influential article in which he addresses humanity's fundamental attitude toward nature and how it developed. He discusses such fundamental questions: Are human beings a part of nature or above it? Is nature's primary value in what we can get out of it—things like natural resources or raw materials—or does it have intrinsic value?

Because of their history, White claims Western nations have inherited certain presuppositions about the relationship between humanity and the natural world, and he thinks these presuppositions can be traced back to Christianity. To support his claim, he turns to Genesis 1—2, and writes, "Man named all the animals, thus establishing his dominance over them. God planned all of this explicitly for man's benefit and rule: no item in the physical creation had any purpose save to serve man's purposes. And, although man's body is made of clay, he is not simply part

of nature: he is made in God's image."[1] Here, White claims
Western Christianity has interpreted Genesis 1:26–27 to
mean that human beings are unique. Among all God's
creatures, only humankind was created in the image of
God. Therefore, we transcend nature. We are separate from
the rest of the natural world and can treat the environment
as it suits us. In the climax of his argument White claims:

> Our science and technology have grown out of
> Christian attitudes toward man's relation to na-
> ture which are almost universally held not only
> by Christians but also by those who fondly regard
> themselves as post-Christians. Despite Coperni-
> cus, all the cosmos rotates around our little globe.
> Despite Darwin, we are not, in our hearts, part of
> the natural process. We are superior to nature, con-
> temptuous of it, willing to use it for our slightest
> whim. The newly elected Governor of California,
> Ronald Reagan, spoke for the Christian tradition
> when he said, "when you've seen one redwood tree,
> you've seen them all." To a Christian, a tree can be
> no more than a physical fact. The whole concept of
> the sacred grove is alien to Christianity and to the
> ethos of the West. For nearly two millennia Chris-
> tian missionaries have been chopping down sacred

---

[1] Lynn White, "The Historical Roots of Our Ecological Crisis," in
This Sacred Earth, 2nd ed. (New York: Routledge, 2003), 197.

groves, which are idolatrous because they assume spirit in nature.[2]

He concludes, "Especially in its Western form, Christianity is the most anthropocentric religion the world has seen."[3]

Although published in 1967, this article still speaks powerfully to our current cultural moment. Introducing the environment in the context of the contemplative life may seem unexpected at first, because mysticism is often thought of as a private, inner journey. The health of the natural world very much relates to the mystical life, however, because mystics do not see themselves as superior to the living things around them; they envision themselves as part of the whole.[4] For example, at the conclusion of his article, White proposes that in a time of ecological crisis the ethos of Francis of Assisi (1181–1226) provides a better role model for the West than the notion of dominion found in Genesis 1. The virtue that White praises in Francis is his humility. Instead of a human "monarchy over creation," Francis promotes a "democracy of all God's creatures."[5] This can be seen in his "Canticle of Brother

---

[2] White, "Historical Roots," 199.

[3] White, "Historical Roots," 197. Anthropocentrism is the belief that human beings are the most significant organisms on the planet and that their interests override those of everything else.

[4] Douglas Christie, *The Blue Sapphire of the Mind: Notes for a Contemplative Ecology* (New York: Oxford University Press, 2013), 34–35, 336.

[5] White, "Historical Roots," 200.

Sun," in which Francis gives familial titles to various features of the natural world. The sun is referred to as "brother" sun. The moon is "sister" moon. Wind and air are "brothers." The earth is our "sister" and our "mother."[6] In other words, sun, moon, stars, wind, air, water, fire, and earth are all part of one family. Francis did not view the creation as a hierarchy with human beings at the top. He saw himself as related to every part of creation. He saw himself as part of a community, a big family of creatures who were all created by God.[7]

THE COSMIC CHRIST

Francis of Assisi is a great example of how mystics don't just connect with God through scripture or contemplation; they also relate to God through the natural world. In his "Canticle," Francis addresses God *through* the various parts of the creation. He writes, "Praised be you, my Lord, through Sister Moon and the stars."[8] For Francis, prayer is not something we only practice with our eyes closed. Here, he doesn't try to rise above material reality in his desire to connect with

---

[6] Francis of Assisi, "The Canticle of Brother Sun," in *Francis and Clare: The Complete Works*, trans. Regis Armstrong and Ignatius Brady (Mahwah, NJ: Paulist Press, 1982), 38–39.

[7] Ilia Delio, *A Franciscan View of Creation: Learning to Live in a Sacramental World* (Bonaventure, NY: The Franciscan Institute, 2003), 10–20; Elizabeth Johnson, *Ask the Beasts: Darwin and the God of Love* (New York: Bloomsbury, 2014), 260–86.

[8] Francis of Assisi, "Canticle," 38.

God. Instead, he pursues God precisely through the natural world. Every part of creation is an icon or sacrament through which we experience the Creator.

Nature mystics like Francis can approach God through the creation because Christ is present within it. Scripture supports this claim. For example, speaking of Christ, Saint Paul states: "him who fills all in all" (Eph 1:23). The *Wilton Translation* makes the "all in all" more specific and renders it as: "him who fills the universe in all its parts."[9] This verse isn't saying that Jesus of Nazareth fills the universe. It is talking about the *cosmic* Christ, the Logos who "was in the beginning with God" (Jn 1) and "is the firstborn of all creation" (Col 1:15). The Franciscan tradition emphasizes this understanding of Christ in contrast to Anselm of Canterbury's (1033–1109) understanding of incarnation. As opposed to Anselm's view that justice demanded Christ, the God-man, had to come to satisfy the besmirched honor of God because of humanity's vast debt of sin, the Franciscan doctrine of the primacy of Christ claims that the principal reason Christ came was "love, not sin."[10] Incarnation was intended from the beginning, not as a remedy for human sinfulness.

Instead of supplying a solution to the problem of sin, the doctrine of the primacy of Christ maintains that the

---

[9] Clyde Wilton, *The Wilton Translation of the New Testament* (Bloomington, IN: Trafford, 2012). Other related texts include Colossians 1:15–17; Ephesians 4:6; and Colossians 3:11.

[10] Ilia Delio, *Christ in Evolution* (Maryknoll, NY: Orbis Books, 2008), 55.

Word is the model or blueprint for the created universe (cf. Jn 1:3; Col 1:15–17). Creation, therefore, is an outgrowth of incarnation. This means that the Word occupies a midpoint between the Father and the world. As Ilia Delio notes: "Thus, as the Word is the inner self-expression of God, the created order is the external expression of the inner Word. The created universe, therefore, possesses in its inner constitution a relation to the uncreated Word."[11] According to Pierre Teilhard de Chardin (1881–1955), Christ is present as the deepest "withinness" of matter. Similar to the way the inner "I" of every human being is Christ and is shared by each person, as we saw in Chapter 7, Christ is also the withinness of every other created thing in the cosmos. So, while everything maintains its external particularity, the "body" of the universe is at the same time also the Body of Christ.[12]

Teilhard's understanding of incarnation can most memorably be seen in his cosmic vision of the Eucharist. Teilhard was a Jesuit and a paleontologist who brought his scientific passion for the natural world to his spiritual writings. Once, on a Sunday when the gospel reading was the story of Christ's transfiguration, Teilhard was on an expedition in a remote Chinese desert. Unable to celebrate mass because he did not have any bread or wine, he imagined what saying mass would be like if he used

---

[11] Delio, *Christ in Evolution*, 59.
[12] Delio, *Christ in Evolution*, 57.

different elements. In his essay "The Mass on the World" he describes the world as an altar on which he offers up the physical processes of growth and diminishment as a sacrifice to God.[13] Instead of bread and wine he offers up all the forces of life and death at work in the world. As he consecrates these elements, he says, "This is my Body" and "This is my Blood."[14] And, with that, Teilhard envisions fire, which represents the Spirit, lighting "up the whole world from within."[15] He describes the penetration of the world by fire: "All things individually and collectively are penetrated and flooded by it. . . . One might suppose the cosmos to have burst spontaneously into flame."[16]

In "The Mass on the World" Teilhard provides a beauti-ful poetic vision of incarnation. In his imaginative reinter-pretation of the eucharistic rite the elements are not the customary ones of bread and wine. Instead, he consecrates the two forces of nature, and the entire cosmos is trans-formed into the body of Christ. This striking visual image expresses his conviction that Spirit is present in matter. It affirms that the incarnation extends into every corner of

---

[13] Thomas King points out that Teilhard does not offer up the entire world in his imaginative celebration of the mass. Rather, he offers up the forces of growth and diminishment, while the world serves as the altar. Thomas M. King, *Teilhard's Mass: Approaches to "The Mass on the World"* (Mahwah, NJ: Paulist Press, 2005), 135.

[14] Pierre Teilhard de Chardin, "The Mass on the World," in *Hymn of the Universe* (New York: Harper and Row, 1965), 23.

[15] Teilhard, "Mass on the World," 23.

[16] Teilhard, "Mass on the World," 23–24.

the universe. It announces that Christ's presence can be seen shining forth from the center of everything in creation if we have eyes to see.

DEEP INCARNATION

A related view of Christ's presence in the natural world is deep incarnation. Elizabeth Johnson notes that John 1:14 does not say that the Word (who was in the beginning with God) simply became a human being, but became *sarx*, a Greek word that is often translated as "flesh."[17] This implies that the Word not only became an individual person but, more broadly, united with all material reality. Niels Gregersen coined the term "deep incarnation" to emphasize the extent of Christ's immersion in matter.[18] God did not simply create the world from outside of it; God in Christ assumed flesh, flesh that shares the same biological components and processes as the rest of the natural world. Therefore, the flesh that Jesus became is made of the same stuff as everything else in the cosmos and is intimately connected with it. As Johnson explains,

> Deep incarnation understands John 1:14 to be saying that the *sarx* which the Word of God became not only weds Jesus to other human beings in the species;

---

[17] Johnson, *Ask the Beasts*, 195.

[18] Niels Gregersen, "The Cross of Christ in an Evolutionary World," *Dialog: A Journal of Theology* 40, no. 3 (Fall 2001): 192–207.

> it also reaches beyond us to join him to the whole biological world of living creatures and the cosmic dust of which they are composed. The incarnation is a cosmic event.[19]

Christ's connection to every atom in the universe has implications for how we treat the natural world. Once we understand the concept of deep incarnation, pursuing our own personal salvation doesn't go far enough. God desires abundant life not just for human beings, but for the entire creation. Today, however, a pervasive anthropocentric attitude separates human beings from the natural world and encourages us to exploit it for our convenience and economic benefit. The concept of deep incarnation helps us see that when we overuse the earth's resources and contaminate its environment, we harm the body of Christ. And when we harm the body of Christ, we harm ourselves, because everything is connected in Christ's body.

ATTENTION

Beatrice Bruteau (1930–2014) defines sin as the failure to recognize the presence of God in the other.[20] *Attention*, therefore, is the spiritual discipline that connects the theological concept of deep incarnation to the everyday life of

---

[19] Johnson, *Ask the Beasts*, 197.

[20] Beatrice Bruteau, *God's Ecstasy: The Creation of a Self-Creating World* (New York: Crossroad, 1997), 173.

the mystic. If God is present in everything, why are we in such a hurry? How can we be so oblivious to God's presence in nature all around us? Let us now focus on three mystics who have written about this discipline of attention. The first is Simone Weil, who addresses the importance of attention in her essay "Reflections on the Right Use of School Studies with a View to the Love of God." For her, "Attention consists of suspending our thought, leaving it detached, empty, and ready to be penetrated by the object."[21] For Weil, self-emptying is essential in any act of attention. She refers to the process of self-emptying as "decreation." We must decreate ourselves, or interrupt our constant stream of thoughts, in order to create mental space to receive the object of attention. She explains, "Attention alone—that attention which is so full that the 'I' disappears—is required of me."[22] Only when we have thus prepared ourselves to receive an object of attention can we affirm, with Weil, that "attention, taken to its highest degree, is the same thing as prayer."[23]

Jesuit scholar Walter Burghardt (1914–2008) defines contemplation as a "long loving look at the real."[24] A

---

[21] Simone Weil, "Reflections on the Right Use of School Studies with a View to the Love of God," in *Waiting for God* (New York: Harper and Row, 1951), 111.

[22] Simone Weil, *Gravity and Grace* (Lincoln: University of Nebraska Press, 1997), 171–72.

[23] Weil, *Gravity and Grace*, 170.

[24] Walter Burghardt, "Contemplation: A Long Loving Look at the Real," *Church* (Winter 1989): 15.

quick look is different from really seeing. In order for our attention to transform into prayer, our gaze needs to linger lovingly on an object. No one embodies this better than our second mystic, Mary Oliver (1935–2019). Oliver celebrated the practice of attending closely to the natural world in her poetry for decades. In poems like "The Summer Day," "Praying," and "Terns," she explicitly connects attention with prayer as she describes specific mundane details she noticed in her practice of attending lovingly to nature, including observations about how the jaws of a grasshopper move and the beauty of white birds that sweep over the waves at the seashore.[25]

The third mystic, Douglas Christie, is a scholar of early desert monasticism. He connects this rich literature with his own experiences of the natural world. For the desert monks like Evagrius, whom Christie studies, it is important to maintain an inner vigilance over our thoughts. The practice of keeping close watch over our thoughts in order to prevent the mind from grabbing a thought and whipping it up into an inner video or commentary must be established before we can attend to the world around us. As we noted earlier with Simone Weil, we cannot give our attention to what is outside of us if we are wrapped up in our own inner chatter. Building on this insight from

---

[25] Mary Oliver, "The Summer Day," in *New and Selected Poems, Volume One* (New York: Beacon Press, 1992), 94; idem, "Praying," in *Thirst* (New York: Beacon Press, 2006), 37; idem, "Terns," in *New and Selected Poems, Volume Two* (New York: Beacon Press, 2007), 34–35.

the desert monks, Christie argues that the contemplative tradition offers resources that are well suited to address the ecological crisis we currently face. Eventually, contemplative practice clears away the mental obstacles that prevent us from living in simple awareness of the presence of God. It facilitates consciousness of living within the whole. Therefore, contemplation provides an opportunity "to know oneself not as a solitary, autonomous being, but as one whose identity can only be conceived as existing within an encompassing web of intricate relationships."[26] The cultivation of such knowledge offers us the opportunity to overcome our fundamental alienation from nature. It provides resources we can use to imagine our relationship to the natural world differently. Thus equipped, our understanding of the goal of contemplative practice broadens. Christie describes this expansion, noting, "The primary work of contemplative practice is to become more aware of this web of relationships, to learn to live within it fully and responsibly, and to give expression to it in one's life."[27]

To illustrate how contemplative practice can help us value the world more deeply, Christie incorporates into his writing an array of quotations and lines of poetry he has gleaned from his wide reading on contemporary nature writing. One thing that stands out in this literature is the

---

[26] Douglas Christie, "The Blue Sapphire of the Mind: Christian Contemplative Practice and the Healing of the Whole," *Sewanee Theological Review* 54, no. 3 (Pentecost 2011): 240–41.

[27] Christie, "The Blue Sapphire of the Mind," 241.

careful attention these authors pay to particular details in nature. We don't live in the world in general. We live in a specific region and place. The level of attentiveness writers and poets such as Mary Oliver exhibit opens them to relationship with the nonhuman world and encourages responsibility for its well-being. And as we read their words, we are challenged to look more closely at the pockets of nature we encounter in our daily lives and cultivate similar levels of attention and intimacy.

BEGIN WHERE WE ARE

Finally, contemporary writers such as Belden Lane and Douglas Christie have written powerfully about the relationship among place, wilderness, and spirituality.[28] The majority of people in the world today, however, dwell in cities and can't travel to places of stunning natural beauty very easily. Most people must access nature close to where they live, myself included. Therefore, parks have become essential to my own spiritual practice in my urban neighborhood.

For the past eight years I have lived in a small one-bedroom apartment with my wife and young son on the Upper West Side of Manhattan. For some, traffic congestion is the major headache in their daily commute. The overcrowding I experience on the sidewalks can be

---

[28] Belden Lane, *The Solace of Fierce Landscapes: Exploring Desert and Mountain Spirituality* (New York: Oxford University Press, 1998); Christie, *The Blue Sapphire of the Mind.*

overwhelming. Since the sidewalks are so crowded, the *way* people walk becomes important. Many, however, are not paying attention to their fellow pedestrians as they move through the space. Tourists look up at the buildings. A person may dart in front of another at any moment; someone directly ahead might suddenly stop to check something on a mobile phone.

Places can shape us positively; we can also be formed otherwise. As I go about my daily errands, I occasionally experience frustration simply navigating the sidewalk in my neighborhood. Sometimes, the unpredictable pace and behavior of those with whom I share the sidewalk pressure me to walk faster than I would prefer. Consequently, I find myself annoyed and irritated with inattentive walkers around me.[29] At times, it is a challenge not to become angry when someone steps in front of me or cuts me off.

There are so many people here that I often feel as though I am locked with those around me in a fierce competition for space. In contrast to the limited space found in my apartment or on the sidewalk, one place I can go to enjoy some room to breathe is a park.

I am fortunate to live within a short walk of Central Park. It was designed by Frederick Law Olmsted to bring the landscape of the countryside to the city, and it certainly feels that way. Because I am drawn to trees, I often head

---

[29] Jen Carlson, "Pedestrian Etiquette 101: How Not to Be a Jerk on the Sidewalk," *Gothamist*, May 16, 2013; Marc Santora, "Think You Own the Sidewalk? Etiquette by New York Pedestrians Is Showing a Strain," *New York Times*, July 16, 2002.

to the same section of the park. The Ramble is a densely wooded section located just north of the Lake. North from the Lake the ground rises in elevation. The Ramble's northern border is marked by Belvedere Castle, which sits atop the second-highest point in the park. The Ramble contains dense forest, a small pond, a meandering stream, rocks to climb, and numerous pathways and benches. The secret of the space is its design. In contrast to Manhattan's street grid, the Ramble contains an incoherent maze of pathways that serves to disorient visitors and consequently make them feel that they are in a much bigger space than it actually is. Despite having visited this section of the park numerous times, it is still difficult to know exactly where I am. The genius of the Ramble's design makes a person feel miles away from the city even though one is actually right in the middle of it.

In this chapter we have explored different aspects of seeking God through the natural world. In my own practice, what connects the environment and mysticism is how being in nature changes the often fraught relationship with obsessive thoughts. When I spend most of my time indoors, the building functions as a "lid" that traps my thoughts inside my head. It makes ordinary responsibilities seem more pressing than they are. When I get outside under the trees, my relationship with my own thoughts changes. Instead of brooding over one concern or another, I am able to release them more easily. In nature I don't cling to my thoughts; they effortlessly escape like carbon dioxide bubbles emerging out of a freshly opened bottle of soda.

What does this look like in my everyday life? When I enter the Ramble in Central Park, I immediately feel myself slow down. I feel calmer and more relaxed. Things on my to-do list seem less urgent. I ruminate less on things that are not going as well as they might be. Escaping the crowds, I live less on the level of the external, superficial self. I feel closer to my center. Being in nature transports me to a different mental space that enables me to let go of thoughts that create the illusion of separation from God and other people. It facilitates a transition from a cluttered mind full of stress and anxiety to a calmer one that feels connected to the whole.[30]

---

[30] For a longer discussion of this topic, see Chad Thralls, "Urban Parks as Sacred Places: Pilgrimage, Solitude, and Access to Nature," *Studies in Spirituality* 28 (2018): 211–31.

Conclusion

In an attempt to communicate the Christian concept of sin to contemporary society, Paul Tillich (1886–1965) likened it to separation.[1] *Separation* is an apt term to describe what afflicts society today. Human beings are separated from themselves, from one another, from the natural world, and from God.

The mystical element of Christianity offers resources to address each of these types of alienation. It is an under-utilized resource that offers fresh ways for Christians to understand their faith and put it into practice. Mysticism is only one element of religion, but it is an essential one. Without the fresh life and energy it provides, religion can become stale or dogmatic. Bernard McGinn defines mysticism like this: "The mystical element in Christianity is that part of its beliefs and practices that concerns the preparation for, the consciousness of, and the reaction to what can be described as the immediate

---

[1] Paul Tillich, *The Shaking of the Foundations* (New York: Charles Scribner's Sons, 1948), 154.

or direct presence of God."[2] In this definition McGinn insists that mysticism, properly conceived, includes more than just powerful experiences. Mysticism is more than just a new feeling; it is a process, journey, or way of life. All the discipline and training in preparation to receive such an experience, as well as the transformed life that is a fruit of the encounter, is properly understood as mystical. When we talk about mysticism, we are not simply interested in experiences, no matter how profound. It is not about temporary states but the entire itinerary mystics follow in their journey to God.

In the course of this book we have outlined different facets of the contemplative path. As we have seen, scripture plays a central role. To explain the depths of spiritual meaning available in the biblical text, Origen made a distinction between the letter and the spirit of the text. Inspired by Matthew 13:44, he thinks there is buried treasure present in scripture that diligent readers seeking God's word *for them* through the text can find. Many mystics in the tradition have approached the story of the bridegroom and bride in the Song of Songs as an allegory of God's passionate love for the soul.

Mystics use two primary modes of language, cataphatic and apophatic, to describe who God is. Cataphatic language uses images of God from scripture, liturgy, and tradition to make the Divine easier to relate to. Apophatic

---

[2] Bernard McGinn, *The Essential Writings of Christian Mysticism* (New York: Modern Library, 2006), xiv.

language, in contrast, emphasizes that God cannot be fully known and that images conceal more about God than they reveal.

Origen believed that human beings are composed of two parts, an inner and an outer. Thomas Merton presents a psychological model of these two aspects of the human person through his metaphor of the true and false self. For Merton, to know our true self is not to uncover some unchanging core of the personality through self-reflection. Essentially, to know the true self is to stop identifying with our external identity and, through the practice of contemplation, receive the awareness that God is our deepest center. Therefore, the true self is not a thing; it is an experience. The false self is the exterior, surface, or superficial self, the self that finds its identity in how it differs from other selves. The false self is a set of mental habits that obscures our awareness of the divine light that is always shining. The goal of the spiritual life is to release these mental habits so the true self can become aware of its innate connection to God.

What makes the practice of contemplation challenging is that as soon as we take away our normal distractions, a steady stream of thoughts seek our attention. Contemplation, then, first requires that we resist the temptation to reach out and grab these thoughts. With practice the mind eventually becomes less dominated by this inner "clutter."

The final chapter considered how mystics understand themselves to be related to the natural world. Introducing the environment in the context of the contemplative life may seem unexpected at first because mysticism is often thought of as a private, inner journey. The health of the natural world very much relates to the mystical life, however. Mystics do not see themselves as superior to the living things around them; rather, they envision themselves as part of the whole. They understand Christ to be present within the natural world, give their careful attention to specific elements of it, develop concern for its well-being, and connect to God through it.

In this book we have explored the mystical element of Christianity as a source of renewal for the tradition. The contemplative path can help us become aware of the ineffable Mystery that is the ground of our being. It is a means of recognizing the small ego-self out of which we normally live so we can connect with the presence of God within us. And despite the concerns of those who criticize spirituality as individualistic, when we loosen our attachment to our own mental drama through contemplative practice, we actually become more free to notice and respond to the needs around us.

We have examined scripture and the contemplative tradition for evocative images and metaphors that can help us reenvision who God is and how we relate to God, other people, and the natural world. These images are not a definitive map; they are trail markers in a dense forest that show us how great hikers before us have traveled.[3]

---

[3] Martin Laird, *Ocean of Light: Contemplation, Transformation, and Liberation* (New York: Oxford University Press, 2019), 181.

At the same time, these metaphors and images are not an alternative set of beliefs. The point of being religious is not to *believe* certain things; it is to deepen our consciousness of God's presence. The primary goal of this book is to help readers come to know the contemplative life by experiencing it for themselves. Jesus articulates the goal of the spiritual life this way: "And they shall be all taught by God" (Jn 6:45). Taste and see. Renew the practice of *lectio divina* and contemplation and thereby experience the life-giving awareness of God to which the mystics testify.

In *Chapters on Prayer* Evagrius writes, "Go, sell your possessions and give to the poor, and take up your cross so that you can pray without distraction."[4] Here Evagrius alters the ending of Matthew 19:21 to make a point about what it means to follow Christ. For him, we follow Christ by engaging in a life of committed contemplative practice. We "sell our possessions" and "take up our cross" by resisting the temptation to grasp onto our constant stream of involuntary thoughts. We follow Christ by cultivating a clear mind (or a pure heart). When our minds have been "decluttered" through contemplative practice, we prepare ourselves to receive the flow of love that God is constantly pouring into the world. Contemplation opens us to receive the love of God, not for ourselves alone, but so that we can pass on the love we have received to those in need.

---

[4] Evagrius Ponticus, *The Praktikos and Chapters on Prayer*, ed. John Eudes Bamberger (Kalamazoo, MI: Cistercian Publications, 1972), 58, no. 17.

Speaking about mysticism, Bernard McGinn says:

> I think the best way to look at mysticism is to speak
> of it as the search for a deeper awareness and con-
> sciousness of God's presence in your life. And that's
> the original meaning of the word *mystic,* which
> means "hidden." God is hidden in everything—
> hidden in us, hidden in the world. And the mystic
> is the person who is seeking to find God, the God
> who is often hidden in a deeper and a more trans-
> formative way. So in that sense mysticism is really an
> integral part of religion. It's not some kind of very
> *special* thing for a *few* people. I think every Christian,
> every baptized Christian, is called to find God as
> deeply as they can in their own lives, and that's what
> I think mysticism is.[5]

It is my hope that this book has provided its readers
with fresh eyes to see God hidden in the Bible, in themselves, in their neighbor, and in the natural world.

---

[5] Bernard McGinn, "What Is Mysticism?" interview (May 21,
2013), https://www.youtube.com/watch?v=3bwLUiZj1Tk.

Select Bibliography

Chariton, Igumen, ed. *The Art of Prayer: An Orthodox Anthology*. New York: Farrar, Straus, and Giroux, 1966.

Christie, Douglas. *The Blue Sapphire of the Mind: Notes for a Contemplative Ecology*. New York: Oxford University Press, 2013.

Dupre, Louis, and James Wiseman, eds. *Light from Light: An Anthology of Christian Mysticism*. 2nd ed. Mahwah, NJ: Paulist Press, 2001.

Gregory of Nyssa. *The Life of Moses*. Mahwah, NJ: Paulist Press, 1978.

Harmless, William. *Mystics*. New York: Oxford University Press, 2008.

———. "The Sapphire Light of the Mind: The *Skemmata* of Evagrius Ponticus." *Theological Studies* 62 (2001): 498–529.

Laird, Martin. *Into the Silent Land: A Guide to the Christian Practice of Contemplation*. New York: Oxford University Press, 2006.

———. *A Sunlit Absence: Silence, Awareness, and Contemplation*. New York: Oxford University Press, 2011.

———. *An Ocean of Light: Contemplation, Transformation, and Liberation*. New York: Oxford University Press, 2019.

Lane, Belden. *The Solace of Fierce Landscapes: Exploring Desert and Mountain Spirituality*. New York: Oxford University Press, 1998.

McGinn, Bernard. *The Essential Writings of Christian Mysticism*. New York: Modern Library, 2006.

———. *The Mystical Thought of Meister Eckhart: The Man from Whom God Hid Nothing*. New York: Crossroad, 2001.

McGuckin, John. *Illumined in the Spirit: Studies in Orthodox Spirituality*. Yonkers, NY: St. Vladimir's Seminary Press, 2017.

———. *Standing on God's Holy Fire: The Byzantine Tradition*. Maryknoll, NY: Orbis Books, 2001.

Merton, Thomas. *New Seeds of Contemplation*. New York: New Directions, 1961.

———. *Thomas Merton: Selected Essays*. Edited by Patrick O'Connell. Maryknoll, NY: Orbis Books, 2013.

———. *Thomas Merton: Spiritual Master. The Essential Writings*. Edited by Lawrence Cunningham. Mahwah, NJ: Paulist Press, 1992.

Ponticus, Evagrius. *The Praktikos and Chapters on Prayer*. Edited by John Eudes Bamberger. Collegeville, MN: Cistercian Publications, 1972.

Schneiders, Sandra. *Women and the Word: The Gender of God in the New Testament and the Spirituality of Women.* Mahwah, NJ: Paulist Press, 1986.

Mechthild of Magdeburg. *Mechthild of Magdeburg: The Flowing Light of the Godhead.* Translated by Frank Tobin. Mahwah, NJ: Paulist Press, 1997.

Index